When Leaving is the Answer

Stories of separation, break ups, and divorce

When Leaving is the Answer
© 2025
ISBN: 9781966337256
First Edition, 2025

Printed in the United States of America

Edited by: Cherice Cameron

Cover Design by: Erica Castro

Layout Design by: Erica Castro

We dedicate this book to all the men and women who have had to navigate the difficulties of a break up, separation or divorce. We know what it is like. We know it is not easy and we see you. May you find bits of hope and light in our personal journey and story. Sending much love.

Disclaimer

The content of this book is for informational and educational purposes only. This book may offer resources, self-realization exercises, suggestions, and ideas that worked for us as individuals. In no way, are we saying that our journey to healing is the only way. The information in this book is intended for educational and informational purposes only. Niether the authors in this book, or the publisher make any represtantations as to the safety of the practices set forth in this book. If you have questions or concerns, please consult a licensed medical professional. The suggestions and resources in this book should not be taken as medical or health advice. They are mere suggestions based on what worked for us as individuals.

Letter to the Reader

Dear Reader,

We have written this book so that people can have an understanding that letting go of difficult relationships is a battle, and it is a battle that you do not have to walk alone. Every person in this book was filled with doubt, fear, and deep insecurities. A lot of us were alone in the process of leaving and divorce, and we asked so many people for answers and advice. We did not know what to do, and we were lost in trying to make the choice of leaving and letting go. Letting go, breaking up, and separating is very hard, but we want you to know that you matter. Your happiness matters, your peace matters, and you deserve to love yourself and put yourself first. Walking away is hard when there are children, homes, and so many things intertwined together, but there is no price for your peace of mind. We are sorry you are here reading this book, but we encourage you to shift your perspective and accept that this is not an ending it is a beginning. Some of us were left, and regardless of the hurt, we did not want a divorce, but today our divorce is the biggest blessing of our life. In ending the relationship, we have been able to discover who we are as human beings, and rise above the break up. This anthology is not only about endings—it's about transformation. It is about breaking cycles rooted in the past, learning to stand in our truth, and remembering that love begins with ourselves. We are sending you prayers, hope, and love. You are not alone, and we wholeheartedly believe in you.

With so much love,

Authors

Table of Contents based on Authors:

Chapter 1

Survival Mode to Empowerment

Ever since I was a little girl, I was desperate for love. I lost my mom when I was five years old and my father had difficulty coping with life resulting in a drinking problem. My father was there for me as best he could, but his grief was overpowering, and he struggled to be emotionally present. Due to the loss of my mother, and my father's coping struggles, I was desperate for someone to pay attention to me. Desperate for someone to love me. If a man looked at me a certain way, I would have a crush on him because of his kindness. Due to the fact that my father had to work, we were often left with baby sitters who had teenage sons. I was victimized, molested on several different occasions, by different teenagers.

The abandonment, loneliness, the shame, and the guilt I carried would dictate the decisions I made in future relationships. Today, I believe that brokenness attracts brokenness. I was a magnet for boys, and men, who would eventually betray me. I had opportunities with kind men but because I was used to abuse, I gravitated towards relationships that would validate my low self-worth. I repeated childhood patterns because that is what felt like home to me. The life I knew as normal.

In repeating childhood experiences, I continually found unavailable men to love, and eventually I met and married my now ex-husband, a marriage that became a dysfunctional rollercoaster and lasted seventeen years. The sparks we shared in the beginning were magical. Now I realize the magic was him highlighting the familiarity of my family's dysfunction. He had so many similarities to my father. I was subconsciously hooked. Today I know that my dysfunctional patterns were in place to prove that if this man could love me, my father was wrong, I was worthy enough to be loved. The problem was that two highly dysfunctional people sometimes bring out the worst in each other. That is what happened to us.

Growing up in a dysfunctional family you learn to have a silent voice, you learn to live in survival mode, and you learn to accept unacceptable behavior. Hope became my addiction, and my ability to always look on the bright side was my enemy. Additionally, indoctrination about divorce was an issue. I was deeply insecure, and desperate for everyone's approval. I could not make my own choices. I asked everybody for advice, yet I could not listen. At the same time, I could not make my own decisions. I failed to determine what was right or wrong. I lived in fear. I was afraid to walk away because I did not know how to handle being alone. I also had the convoluted thought of "if I leave, then my kids will not have a dad." I grew up without a mother and I was afraid of what would happen.

My husband had multiple affairs throughout our marriage, he had an alcohol addiction issue, and he struggled to be in control when he got excessively drunk. I put out fires on a daily basis and he was extremely angry all of the time. We were all walking on eggshells. I constantly cried on my way to work. I was depressed, and I felt lost. I was living in fear, and I did not have the self-esteem to walk away.

In 2010, my husband had an affair. The other affairs he had were mainly physical, but this affair was different, he loved her. I did not understand it, and looking back, I realize I lived in denial. The denial was interesting because my obsession with him was similar to the obsession he had with her. We tried to work it out, but unfortunately I began binge drinking. Alcohol had not been an issue for me previously, but when you play dangerously, you can become addicted. That is what happened to me. I developed a drinking problem. We were still together until 2014, when I finally gave up the house we were renting and found my own apartment. An extremely difficult time, I had no choice. Living with him had become unbearable. He did not respect me. Other women would pick him up at all hours of the day or night regardless of my being home or not.

One time, I literally wanted to kill him. But by the grace of God I left the relationship without physically hurting him. I was at work when his brother called me and said my dog got out. I called my husband, and told him the dog got out. The "other" woman was loud, so I could hear her voice. I felt crazy, and I wanted to hurt him physically. I was done at work, and I was speeding home. I imagined hurting him. All of a sudden, I remembered a line in a book that I had read so many years ago. The story was about a woman who was married to a serial cheater. She wrote that she knew she had lost control the moment she was chasing her husband around the house with a knife in front of her kids. That thought saved me. I did not go home, instead, I went to meet one of my best friends. I stayed with her until around 9 pm, and I was calm. I had three weeks left to move to my apartment. All I needed to do was to be patient and control my emotions.

Eventually, we left each other for several months, and eventually I was back on the roller coaster. We lived separately, trying to fix things, but the bottom line was he had never gotten over the other woman. He loved her. Obsessed about her. However, since I was in my own apartment, I set very clear boundaries. The apartment was mine, and I was very clear to say "if you are going to be here and act emotionally distant or not present, you can go." I did not lose my temper or control. I knew what he was capable of, so this time it was different. I had built some self-esteem, and I was sober. Nothing was more important to me than my sobriety because in sobriety I was giving my children stability. We had some good times together, and some peace. I had changed, but it was not enough for us to heal our marriage. The thing my ex-husband left me was my strong intuition, and how to study people's behaviors.

In December, I had another birthday. I remember praying and asking "please God if he is not for me, then make this end." I did not want to waste anymore years with a man who was not vested in me. In two weeks, I noticed his behavior changing, and I knew he was talking to the other woman again. I was hurt. At the same time, I had prayed for an answer. I was calm and collected. I packed the little things he had at my apartment, drove all the way to his work, and told him in a kind, nice way that I had a surprise for him. He emptied his car so I could surprise him. I left his box with a letter saying that I wish it works out for them, and I hope he finds what he is looking for. The following month I filed for divorce and hoped that would be the end of the journey, but it was not.

I would eventually try and work it out again. Again he went back to the other woman. It was not until he finally was honest enough to tell me, "Erica, the best thing you could do is find someone else, divorce me, I don´t love you the same." I needed him to tell me that, and that was really the end for us. I was heavily criticized for not letting go sooner. All I can say to that is "you learn when you learn."

The divorce was difficult because initially he asked for so much. He wanted alimony, he wanted half of my retirement, and he was asking to be the beneficiary for my life insurance. I never realized the vulnerability a person faces during divorce especially after over ten years of marriage. My soon to be ex-husband was entitled to what he was asking, but it was difficult to navigate. Eventually, I stretched out the divorce because I knew he was going to find a woman who would demand that he sign the divorce papers. I was blessed enough to walk away from the marriage completely intact financially.

I started dating. A monumental wake up call. The first man I dated was exactly like my ex-husband. That is when I realized that I was part of the problem. I needed to do monumental healing to be able to receive love and to be a healthy enough partner to have a decent relationship. I did not realize that I was so unbelievably broken that I would attract men who would hurt me. For the first time I dedicated my time to healing the broken parts of myself. I started unpacking my childhood trauma and looking at the dysfunction I brought to the table. I originally chose to stay because I did not know any better, but I knew I could learn a different way of life.

I started reading all of the dating books I could find. I went back to 12-step meetings and started therapy. I needed to heal the parts of myself that did not feel worthy of love. I had to dig deep and look at the moments when I did not feel worthy in my childhood. I needed to discover the things that I let define me growing up. For example, I was bullied in school as a child. Being bullied left a deep mark in my heart because I had begun to define myself by the pain and hurt caused by others. I suffered because I was different. I believed what the bullies said about me, which led me to put myself in compromising situations by chasing people who were incapable of loving me.

I was grateful for my new found knowledge because it gave me some sense of control. I could work on myself and change the trajectory of my life. I could eventually come into a relationship where a person could value and love me. I had to rewrite the narrative and the mental abuse I was constantly feeding to my own mind because of the life I had lived. It took a lot of work, but the one thing I can say is that little by little you can become a completely different person when you do the work to heal, and understand why you are the way you are. It was a struggle for me, but I have transformed myself into someone who loves herself today.

I constantly work on becoming the best version of myself. I do the work because I want to continue growing and transforming. It is important to avoid stagnation and try something new. The best therapy I have ever received came from writing my books, collaborative chapters, poetry, and by speaking my own truth. It is so important to let every thing out. By writing your story you can help heal others. I write in the hopes that someone out there can feel less alone because I know what it feels like to be in their circumstances.

Regarding the divorce, I would say divorce is always a hard decision. Divorce for me was the biggest blessing for my life. I would not have been able to do half the things I have been able to do if I did not divorce. When I finally stopped living in survival mode, I felt a sense of peace and understanding that I had never had before. I have grown into a person who is able to make sense of life, and I am also able to be present in my kids' lives. I have been able to stay sober, and navigate my life in an effective way.

My divorce was difficult because my ex wanted a lot from me, but once he found another person, she convinced him to sign the divorce papers. I am forever grateful to her because she set me free from the legal entanglement with my ex-husband. It took a long time for me to divorce, but he let me go. He did not fight for my retirement, and he did not ask for alimony, so I was very grateful.

My advice to all the people who are going through this is to journal. A lot of our emotions can become out of control causing bitterness and anger. While these emotions are necessary, it is important not to allow the emotions to dominate and control your mindset. A lot of us are victims of abuse or infidelity, or both, and we are suffering trauma because of our marriage. I can tell you that bitterness and meanness will not help you. You have to work on forgiving yourself and letting go. When you are consumed with bitterness it takes away from your life. You have a right to be angry, process those emotions and navigate your way through them. Hurt people hurt others, and dysfunctional people can be hurtful, so find your own way to heal, and try to live in gratitude.

This part of your life; however grim, can give you an opportunity to have a new life and can lead to growth and new perspective. I can honestly say that the divorce was one of the biggest blessings of my life. When you stop living in survival mode, there is a sense of empowerment that you can build because you are no longer under someone else's foot. I dedicated myself to healing and working on myself, and through this process I was able to write in several book collaborations, write three books, speak on online platforms, and start a publishing company. I could not have done this without being free from abuse. Little by little, I have raised my self-esteem, and I am doing things that fill my heart.

I have done all kinds of things in the quest for healing. I have learned to meditate, journal, and I have found support in 12-step programs, breathwork, and therapy. The one thing I can honestly say is that other than doing Witality breathwork, nothing has healed me like writing books. Writing has pulled a lot of the pain out of my body and has allowed me to reach a point of acceptance. I want you to know that in order for new doors to open, you have to close the doors that take peace from you. Close those doors that no longer serve you. As much as you want something to happen in your life, for example; I wanted to stay married, letting go will give you the greatest freedom. I have freedom that I never would have found had I not divorced. Divorce was truly the biggest blessing of my life.

The Enabling Dance

He kissed me and I wanted to throw up
It is just a temporary band-aid
Eventually, he will strip off
With no gentleness

Until the next falling out
Of you did this to me
So I did this to you
Never-ending swirl

Cataract eyes
I fail to see what is in front of me
I see blotches and shades
But is not clear

My eyes
Connected to the heart
It is my denial
that keeps me
on this emotional train

I do not want to see the truth
He is sometimes nice

Repeated childhood bonds
That is what this is
Dysfunction
No one learns boundaries
in chaos
No one learns to love
in abuse

It teaches
once in a while type of love

The one where
Daddy is in a good mood
So he shows kindness
Temporary
Short-lived

'Til Dad's alcohol
drowns
love
clouds it
confuses it
lowers my self-worth

Childhood bonds
That live in adulthood
That jade my choices
That makes you love potential

Childhood bonds

That makes me still
cry for you
You left me
so long ago
when you died

For years
I just wanted
a fraction
a word
a glance

And today
All I want is him
My cohabitant
We live together
But we are trapped
In a dance

I will not leave
Neither will he
I enable
He enables

Stuck
Empty
Unfulfilled

Walking on stickers
Fear's victory
We live in quiet desperation

This poem reflects my marriage, and my inability to leave. I was stuck and had a hard time walking away from what was familiar to me. The unknown was scary, but what I can say in retrospect is that you can have an amazing life, if you just heal and let go of what no longer serves you. I also learned that these patterns came from my childhood, and not feeling good enough, so I had to work on myself. The biggest wake up call for me was that the first guy I dated was a replica of my ex husband. The guy ghosted me, but what that experience taught me was that I was attracting from a place of low self-worth, and I had to heal all that before I could have a great relationship.

Erica Castro is a veteran English high school teacher. She is a poet that feels that poetry can be a stepping stone for healing. She is currently in the book production of publishing *My Silent Voice Unleashed*. She participated in a book collaboration called *Alive to Thrive*. She is a collaborating author for *Badass Within*, and *Healing and Growth Book* she also has published in the *Graceful Growth*. Her poetry is published in the anthology called *Somos Xicanas*, and her poetry is currently being publishe by Beyond the Veil Press in their Biopic Anthology. She is currently a publisher and just published Rosalilia M. Mendoza's poetry collection *Lili of the Valley* foreword written by *Always Running* author Luis J. Rodriguez. She is focused on publishing students' work. She has published two anthologies for Schurr high school, the school she works at. In 2025, she published 7 different student authors. She is also the founder of Daxson Publishing.

Chapter 2

The British are Coming!

The British are Coming

Part I

When I was 18 years old, I married an Englishman almost twice my age. Why, you ask? Good question. Afterall, I grew up in modern Southern California, not in some other culture or era when marriage at a young age was more standard and perhaps necessary for women. But it was a complicated situation. There was no straight nor easy path for me. But I suppose once you look under the hood of a person's life, nobody really has an easy time of it, do they? Many Gen-Xers like me had to sink or swim. I was an OG latch-key kid, walking or biking home from school, getting my own snacks (i.e. way too much candy), and overseeing my own homework, all before mother and father got home from work. Yes, the Greatest Generation were strong S.O.B.s, but I'll argue all day long that my generation rivals them in both strength of character and making the most of our survival instincts.

One complication was that my parents went through a prolonged and difficult divorce when I was a senior in high school, and despite my honed independence, I was still scared shitless. Their divorce was many years in the making, and I supported it, but it still felt like the bottom had dropped out of my world. Because of the divorce, I did not go away to a four-year university, which had been my dream. After my father left for good to marry a woman 20 years his junior, I stayed with my mother, worked a part-time job, and started at the very good but local community college. My father was also a well-known, tenured professor there. My father's position did not afford me any special perks, but he was familiar with the campus, and it was cheap. It was my only choice. So, I went and made the best of it; I loved learning, and I loved my classes. But my mother was restless, and so was I. I wanted a way out to see the wider world. I've always had the travel bug crawling around inside me. And I knew that I had a lot of unrealized potential, even if I had no distinct plan for unleashing it. Despite my fear, I was still determined to machete a path through the overgrown forest of life. Wild horses couldn't stop me from making something of myself. However, it turned out that they could delay me.

Another complication involved my senior-year, high school boyfriend moving away and dumping me for a sleek, Scandinavian blonde, which was not exactly a self-esteem booster. Most of my close-knit group of high school friends, including my BFF, spread to the winds. As a result of these major coming-of-age shifts, during my first semester in college, I made a series of rapid-fire choices. I thought I was choosing the courses of a grown-up gourmet meal, but it was riddled with poison. Although I'd graduated from high school with a 4.0 and had every intention of going the distance with my education, which I eventually did, I still knew almost nothing about navigating the adult world on my own, despite my Gen-X grit. Going from my mother's house to marriage seemed like a good idea at the time. This wasn't my main motivation for getting married, but in hindsight, it did heavily influence my subconscious. It was certainly a coping strategy. At eighteen what did I know about anything?

Another huge factor was the role religion played in my upbringing. I went to a born-again-style, evangelical Christian high school, which was partly my choice and partly my mother's, but the so-called sex education we received was steeped in what would shortly thereafter be called purity culture. One should save oneself for marriage. But I was extremely ripe to pop my cherry. Many long years of adolescent longing and raging hormones were difficult to contain by that point. Employing sheer stubborn will, I had not given in yet, despite numerous opportunities, but the virginal damn was about to break. Many people around me, including my older brother, had gotten married very young—some were still teenagers.

At age 17, I got my first job, and I've worked ever since. In those days, I got around in a beat-up, rusty old Dodge passed to me from my cousin. Right after I turned 18, I started college and worked as a waitress at a popular restaurant not far from our church. During one lunch shift, I waited on two gentlemen at a two-top table by the front window. I knew one of the men from church—he was a pastor there. The other was a visiting guest speaker. The guest speaker liked the look of me, and I liked his British accent. Oh, and he was a writer, which also appealed to me. I was an outgoing but bookish sort who read voraciously, watched BBC dramas on PBS, and dreamed of being a writer and college professor. I also come from mostly British stock, and to this day, I still have an acute case of Anglophilia. I tried to date boys my own age, but they were desperately immature. I was looking for something different, something exotic, I suppose.

After that brief encounter in the restaurant, it seemed incredible, but the Englishman called our house, asking for me. He must have gotten the number from our mutual church acquaintance. Soon after, he took me on a date to Santa Barbara. In what I now judge as one of her crazier moments, my mother let me go on a date with this much older man! I think she felt guilty about how the divorce affected me and wanted to see me "settled" after my father left. But still! Geesh. What probably clinched it for me was that the Englishman paid me some compliments on my writing. I shared an essay with him about attending my first funeral. Finally! Somebody matched my nerd energy. After that, I was under his thrall. One thing led to another—yada, yada, etc., etc. The Englishman proposed, and we were married before my first year in college was finished. As Jane Austen might phrase it, I was but 18 years old.

Don't get me wrong. I'm not a complete idiot. The Englishman was nice enough in the beginning. We had a good time for the short period of dating and for the first months of marriage. He was on his best behavior to lure me in. We might call it "love-bombing" these days. He took me to the UK and Europe. I was starting to see the world outside my SoCal bubble. Don't get me wrong about this, either. He didn't have money, or anything. There was no revelation that he was actually a prince from some made-up sounding European country, like in a Hallmark movie. No, the Englishman's father had been a prosperous grocer in the North of England and could afford to send his son to what we would call a private prep school and then to university. The Englishman had climbed to middle-class at best, but there was no family money. Overseas, we mostly stayed with his brother and friends and did outings on a shoestring. For example, I saw

31

the outside of the Louvre, but it was many years before I could afford to see the inside of it. But because my teenage life felt stagnated, this seemed like an adventure worth the risk. During our first year of marriage, I went to another full year of college, so by then I had two years under my belt. It was a decent start. To my father's credit (and trust me, he doesn't deserve much), he made me promise to finish college, a value he taught me to respect. No matter what, I wasn't going to disappoint myself on this count.

To date, I have only written about the Englishman in fictionalized accounts. Those stories are based on true events, but I blurred some lines to protect identities and whatnot, and to create coherent narratives. But the following will be as close to the blunt, bare truth as I can mine from my past. It's about damn time. It has been decades, and I try not to think about the worst of what happened. Despite having righted the boat of my life long ago, unbearable memories still wash over me like malicious ghosts. The traces of trauma trail out of a pernicious mist when I least expect them. I must still shout those ghouls down and cast them out more often than I would like. "Be gone!" I demand, like an old-timey preacher casting out the devil.

I was a rule-following, high-achieving, well-meaning, goodie two-shoes kid. I was a genuinely naïve and trusting soul, as my mother was before me. Like her, I believed that most people were decent. I possessed a normal, healthy amount of self-esteem. I naturally expected to be treated with kindness and respect, and to be rewarded for doing my best. Despite my parents' awful marriage, I was still optimistic for myself and my own future, as youth is wont to do. But lacking in experience at such a young age, I had no way of anticipating the Englishman's deeply dysfunctional core character. I mean, what sort of grown man marries an 18-year-old girl? A man with a lot of problems, that's who. Today, I recognize his behavior as predatory, entitled, and narcissistic—at a profoundly pathological level. "Narcissist" and "predator" are commonplace psychobabble labels these days, but he was genuinely troubled. Also, in those days men got away with a lot—society had not properly called them out quite yet. I didn't have a stream of YouTube channels, Tik Tok trends, or Instagram reels to dissect and explain poor male behavior at the touch of a button. I could not have remotely predicted what was to come.

It turned out that the Englishman had deeply ingrained patterns of "burn-this-shit-down" self-destructive behavior. Every time something went well for him, he figured out a way to screw it up—from relationships to jobs. It was like he had a demon on his shoulder, luring him into trouble. He was honest enough with me about his history. He immigrated to America after a job in the U.K. flamed out. He was divorced from wife #1. I was wife #2. He had a green card before he met me, so that wasn't a factor, but trust me, there were plenty of other red flags--in the flush of youth, I was blind to them. Besides, when one is young and inexperienced, one rarely thinks that anything bad will happen to them—bad luck is for other people.

The Englishman wasn't very good with money. He constantly wished for it and worried about it but did little to make any; he only took on jobs he considered worthy of his "talent" (writing, editing, speaking engagements). These jobs do not pay much, unless you are famous on the Stephen King level. He was always waiting for his "big break." He never worked an ordinary job in his life, while I, on the other hand, have done everything you can think of from cleaning houses and babysitting to retail, waitressing, tutoring, painting signs for store windows, and temporary secretarial work. I even clipped an elderly man's toenails! My philosophy is that all work has dignity, and when it is necessary to make money, one needs to do something about it—not just whine about it. Yes, how very Gen-X of me.

It is likely that the Englishman was on the bi-polar spectrum. This condition is known by several terms, including manic-depressive disorder, but I am especially partial to the expression "circular insanity"—one minute over-the-moon with false confidence and the next in a crippling depression topped with explosive outbursts of anger and a paranoia that life "had it in for him." He suffered from headaches, which in hindsight may have been undiagnosed high blood pressure. People often fell over him with deference; a well-spoken, educated Englishman seems so above-board, so trustworthy to us hick Americans. He was used to being fawned over. So, he expected me to buy into all of it, and to follow him down every labyrinthine path, holding space for him at every turn. Not that I don't have compassion for people with mental disorders—it's that I didn't know how to recognize, understand, avoid, and put boundaries around them when I was so young. I didn't deserve to be sucked up into that situation. I didn't deserve to be a victim of his deep dysfunctions. And there was no reciprocity. The Englishman's lack of empathy towards me was astonishing in its breadth. He once told me that a woman's period was natural, so it shouldn't hurt, that I must be imagining things. If I caught a cold, it was somehow my fault. If I stumbled or dropped something, I was clumsy and unladylike. He was never truly concerned about my welfare, and it only went downhill from there.

The Englishman's behavior slowly deteriorated, unraveling before me like a knit sock undone by the devil himself. This unpeeling shook my understanding of the world to its foundations. My father had been no angel, but my father's bad behavior was nothing compared with what the Englishman was capable of.

After we married, the Englishman decided to pursue—wait for it—a degree in divinity so that he could be a Presbyterian pastor. Yep. That's right. A church pastor. At least this was a move towards stability. First, we moved to Palm Springs for his pre-graduate school internship. His northern English hide soaked up the heat like a satisfied lizard, while I hated the desert with a passion—I am NOT a warm-weather person. It was like we had literally moved to hell. We could barely afford anything, especially not air conditioning. Thankfully, after a year, we moved to the San Francisco Bay Area, where I could breathe again, and where he attended a famous Presbyterian seminary. During this time, he continued with his freelanced writing jobs—things like technical writing for catalogs and ghostwriting books for an array of people, including some famous ones, such as one of the Apollo astronauts. Not right away, but in the years ahead, the Englishman became somewhat well-known in the religious, philosophical, and New Age-y self-help world. He even had modest success with a book or two of his own, although money problems have remained a constant for him. He thought he was Eckhardt Tolle, but he was more akin to a bumbling, cruel dictator, some version of Adolf Hitler played in a high-campy style by the likes of Peter Sellers.

When the Englishman started seminary, he became even more utterly self-absorbed, entitled, and domineering. He either sat in an armchair reading like a king on a throne or typing at a computer like some crazed Kafka. He did little else, except eat (a lot), sleep, and attend the occasional class. He not only foisted his writing work onto me and took the credit for it, but he also expected me to wait on him like an old-school servant. From bringing him freshly made juice in bed in the mornings to taking care of all the housework, food shopping and preparation, and paying the bills. In addition to doing his writing jobs, I also had to bring in money through additional part-time jobs, such as cleaning houses and clipping the toenails of an elderly man.

The era of the Englishman's upbringing in Britain instilled in him old-fashioned expectations about marriage. Because I was raised in that fundamentalist Christian environment by a mother brought up in the 1950s, I went along with a lot of it at first, thinking I would be respected and thanked for my diligent work as cook, cleaner, scullery maid, household secretary, hostess to his friends, and a ghostwriter's ghostwriter, all while managing to maintain a 4.0 in community college and holding down part-time jobs. But I couldn't have been more wrong.

Instead of appreciating and cherishing me, all physical contact dried up, and he panicked about each facet of everyday life, all the while severely criticizing everything I did, picking on the tiniest mistake. Even when I was right about things (which, let's face it, ladies, was most of the time), everything made him angry no matter how well I did things. Did I move his book? Did I clean the bathroom? Had I touched the toilet? The very thought of germs freaked him out. Did I do the laundry correctly? Did I buy the organic green beans? He belittled my looks and the way I dressed. Obviously, I did my best on what little we had, but he expected me to look and dress like a fashion model. I was told later that the people who lived in our graduate school apartments could hear him screaming at me every day.

Even before he became overtly violent, he was extremely controlling, wielding manipulation and humiliation like a weapon. Although I only weighed about 110 lbs., he called me fat almost every day. Like literally every man I have been with, he regularly declared, "You're going to get fat like your mother." Of course, every person is a beautiful miracle and perfectly marvelous as they are, but I am taking this opportunity to rub in the face of every man I've been with that I, in fact, have never "got fatten," even these decades later. Take that, all you asshats out there: Lisa *never* "got fat like her mother."

The Englishman insisted that I eat a low-carb diet. He would only have organic food in the house, which we couldn't afford. If I deviated in any way from his prescriptions for grocery shopping, cooking, eating, dressing, behaving, or simply breathing, I was punished. If I didn't buy the correct items, I had to return them. I was not allowed to use the car. I had to bicycle everywhere. He isolated me from my family by telling me what flakes they were, while at the same time pressuring them for money as compensation for "taking me on." If dinner was a minute late on the table, he threw it against the wall, the organic spaghetti noodles and homemade sauce sliding down the wall like a Jackson Pollock painting. He carried on yelling at me while I cleaned it up, his face reddening and arms flapping.

Among these clearly unacceptable behaviors, one of the most irksome was that he took the moral high ground on virtually everything you can think of from organic food, culture, and politics to self-help programs and "spiritual development." He was the very embodiment of the classic, know-it-all "mansplainer." To this day, he remains the biggest hypocrite I have ever known.

He most certainly did not practice what he preached. There was no kindness, no compassion, no consideration for me as a person. I recently read a very insightful article that sums up his relationship to me quite perfectly: men need women, but they don't necessarily like women. Men are not forced to understand, empathize with, or appreciate women. They see women as tools, as a means to an end, as trophies, as reflections of themselves. I recently heard an interview in which a man says that he married a specific woman for "the same reason all men choose a woman—because she was hot." But then, this man was surprised to learn that his wife had a "capacity for reason" and that she was usually right about most things. Holy, fricking moly. And this was in 2024! In my vast experience with men, I know that few of them put in the work to understand and cherish women for the amazing people we are. Clearly, I had started out with very unrealistic and naïve expectations for marriage, which were crushed with a cruel finality under the wheels of the Englishman's dysfunction.

As I write this, my mind has blocked out the very first time the Englishman hit me. Traumatic memories can be elusive creatures, but, like it or not, many, many specific violent incidents remain seared in my memory like a horror film on a loop. Even though this marriage is ancient history, my stomach is in knots as I write this. My hands are clammy, and my anxiety is at a 10 out of 10 on the trauma scale. Here are a few examples of these violent incidents: When necessity required that I learn to drive a stick shift car, instead of carefully explaining and being patient, he would hit my arms as hard as he could with his fists when I made mistakes—while I was driving. My arms were riddled with purple bruises. I wore long sleeved blouses. There were frequent kicking sessions with leather-bottomed shoes. I cowered beside bookcases or hid in closets. My legs were also covered in bruises. I wore long pants year-round. The places he hit me were calculated so that no one could easily see what was happening. For example, he never hit me in the face. That would be too obvious.

One day, I was in the kitchen chopping vegetables. He was yelling at me about God knows what (That he regretted marrying me? That I was getting fat? That I made too many mistakes on a manuscript? That I was running late? That my mother was ridiculous? That the peaches weren't organic so take them back to the store?). I kept my head down, gripping the knife until my knuckles were white with rage. I was merely trying to control myself, my cheeks hot with humiliation and despair. I did not look up or say anything, but he exploded, "So you want to kill me, now? Is that it? You going to stab me with that knife, now?

Are you? Well?!! Pathetic." He grabbed it from my hand and brandished it at me, demonstrating how to wield it. I ran out of the house. What happened next? How did I survive that encounter? I don't remember, exactly. After several hours, I probably slinked back into the house and hid shivering under a blanket, praying that he had calmed down enough to leave me alone for a while.

This type of abuse became an on-going reality for me. But I didn't fight back physically. One of the reasons is that I was taking a high road of my own. I would never harm another human being. Ever. But also, if you've never experienced this kind of abuse, I need to make another thing clear: In this situation, one is so shocked, so frightened, so humiliated, so frozen that it causes a person to shut down to survive her next breath. Then, her next. Not to mention that it is extremely dangerous to antagonize an abuser. I wasn't stupid; I wanted to survive.

Why didn't I leave him then? Afterall, I had plenty of time, a whole life stretching out before me. One reason was that I had no money and nowhere to go. My mother had quit her job and ran off to Texas to live with her sister, my father was re-married, and my brother had his own family and problems.

Besides, the shame of this situation cannot be understated. I made a bold move in marrying at the age of 18, and it most definitely did not work out, as my brother had warned me it probably wouldn't. My brother did not attend my wedding in an act of protest. I still don't know whether my brother did the right thing there, but I certainly could not turn to him—not right away. I couldn't tell anyone what was really happening behind the closed doors of the up-and-coming seminary student.

Again, you ask: Why did I stay? There was an even bigger reason. About 18 months into our relationship, there was an incident with a broken condom. I became pregnant. I intended to wait a good long time, finish college, and start a career before even thinking about a baby, but that is not what happened. That boozy fourth of July afternoon was the very last time the Englishman ever had sex with me. That is why I know exactly when, where, and how it happened. And so, college—and even my very life—was on the backburner for the time being. Survival mode switched into the highest possible gear. Again, as Jane Austen might phrase it, I was but 19 years old.

The pregnancy exacerbated the Englishman's bad behavior. He wanted the baby—that wasn't it—but he most definitely didn't want me. The Englishman lashed out at me in wild fits of anger, all the while attending seminary, accepting baby shower gifts, and welcoming congratulations from his peers and family. Again. Biggest. Hypocrite. Ever. He continued to hit me, lock me out of the house, and force me to ride a bike instead of using the car--yes, even pregnant. More than once, he threw most of my belongings and clothes out the back door. A suitcase was included, which bounced forlornly into the street where it sat like an incongruent object in a Salvador Dali painting.

The numerous, daily acts of cruelty were endless. If I ate anything remotely "bad" for a pregnancy, there was hell to pay. By the way, I did eat a very healthy diet for the baby, but the Englishman's notions were always rather bonkers. Maybe the yogurt culture wasn't strong enough? Couldn't I make my own yogurt from raw milk? As far as he was concerned, I existed only as a broodmare and house servant. And even some sort of chemical magician in the kitchen.

After the baby was born, I had tunnel-vision, focused on motherhood. I breastfed my son until he was two years old. He and I slept on an old mattress in the spare room. I did my best to keep the two of us alive. I took my son to the state-run clinic for his check-ups and vaccinations. There was throw-up on the floor, and it stank of urine. I accepted food stamps. I even managed to take my son to visit my grandmother who lived two hours away. I talked to my mother on the phone when I could. But nobody knew what was really happening. Finally, the day of the Englishman's graduation from seminary was on the horizon. He had gotten a job at a church in another state.

Part II

In 1960, 72% of American adults over the age of 18 were married. In the recent past, American women were basically stuck with the hands they were dealt. Most of them languished at home with no access to decent healthcare or birth control. They had to fight hard to get jobs, education, careers, and financial independence. Heck, women couldn't even get a bank account or a credit card until the early 1970s.

Today, only about 50% of American adults are married. Fewer people are getting married in the first place, but, yes, divorce is also much easier to obtain. There is little judgement, and few consequences attached to it. So, I don't blame the average person for thinking that divorce is a uniquely contemporary issue. But divorce is not a new phenomenon. For example, divorce was simple and commonplace in ancient Rome. If either party wanted to dissolve the marriage, the woman took back her dowry and left. Also, if the male head of a family wanted to place a woman in a more financially or socially advantageous marriage, he could do so on a whim. Emperors such as Octavian Augustus moved women around like chess pieces to increase his power and connections.

In subsequent centuries, marriages were always flexible entities, even when divorce wasn't allowed. For example, what did prominent gay men do? Get married, and then let his wife live her own life, that's what. In most cultures, men have always been allowed—even expected—to have mistresses or concubines. In some cultures, they had multiple wives. The idea that marriage is a sacred, inviolable, monogamous institution between two people is absurd when you start poking into the historical details of how people have handled marriage. I mean, look at Henry VIII? If you had his power, it would be very tempting to lop off a few heads. In the upper classes, people got married and then carried on with whomever they pleased. It was harder for women, but they did it. In the lower classes, people often couldn't afford to get married—they just lived in loosely defined family units and called it a day. And what about all the many, many cultures based on slavery? That topic alone could fill an entire book that someone has probably already written.

Today, there is one big difference, though—women have a wider range of control over their own destinies. Today, a slightly higher percentage of women than men graduate from college. But the greater control women have over their lives still does not make divorce easy. I honestly wouldn't wish divorce on anyone, but sometimes, it is necessary.

Part III

Shortly after the Englishman accepted that church job in another state, I screwed up my courage. I approached his throne-like reading chair, as if I was addressing a monarch. I announced that I was not going with him. I was not going to leave California. At the ripe old age of 22, I would get a scholarship to attend college. He simply replied, "Good." His expression barely changed. He crossed one leg over the other and kept reading. That was all that he ever said about it. Our relationship lasted approximately four years from beginning to end.

As I had no money, no place to go, and no substantial job, in the short-term, I became a live-in caregiver to a quadriplegic woman until I could get some financial aid together to start college. Naturally, at first my emotional and physical state were not good. I have suffered from PTSD twice in my life. The first time occurred after the divorce from the Englishman. I weighed 97 pounds. The bones stuck out from my ribs. I could barely see in front of me, much less see the blue of the sky or the color in flowers. Food tasted like sand, and I had trouble sleeping. I cried a lot, bunched up in the fetal position. I was a wreck. It took a lot of focus, many years, and my Gen-X grit to keep moving forward, inch by inch, headed toward the life I live today.

In the end, I went to four different colleges to graduate Magna Cum Laude with a bachelor's degree in English literature and a minor in drama, which I finished before I turned 25. I was still working as a waitress while I got my teaching credential, but once I finished student teaching, I got temporary teaching positions, and then a full-time job as a high school teacher. But this wasn't enough for me. I wanted to achieve more. I worked full-time teaching high school English while I got my M.A. in literature, so that I could transition to teaching college. Same for getting my doctorate. I taught a full load of college classes while I was in graduate school. It took a long time to pass that final hurdle, but I did it. I finally became Dr. Montagne. I achieved my goals of becoming a college professor, and I'm still hacking away at the writer thing. It's coming along okay enough. (Insert shrug emoji here).

It is a common urban myth and talking point on both

sides of the current political aisles that college is not affordable. The facts are, especially in California, that anybody can do it. While college is certainly not necessary for everyone, literally anybody can at least try. In California, you can start at a community college, which has open enrollment (this means that everyone is accepted at any age), then you can transfer to a trade program or a university and go from there. Yes, you must work hard and get good grades, but it is doable without taking out massive loans. To fund college, I paid with what I gathered from part-time jobs, scholarships, and government grants. I currently have four college degrees, and the most I ever borrowed was $15,000, which I repaid years ago.

No, I didn't go to a fancy ivy league school or end up teaching at an upscale university, although I was a full-time lecturer at the University of California Irvine for three years. That's as far up the ladder I ever got. But I am perfectly happy with my imperfect job teaching community college students. I love them! Yes, today, I am a college English professor. I teach college classes, help students, serve on committees, train faculty, and speak at conferences. I became an educational technology specialist. This means that I train faculty how to use computers for teaching. I was the distance education manager for a college for three years. I've presented countless lectures, seminars, and trainings, to faculty, in addition to my regular teaching load. I've also worked on important issues, such as open educational resources, helping faculty use course design to eliminate textbooks from their curriculum, which saves students money on expensive textbooks. I'm very proud of what I've achieved in my career.

I also teach poetry in a community program and run dance events. I love going to high tea with my friends, giving themed parties, and making costumes. I've traveled to at least 11 countries and 26 states, and I love creating art and decorating my home. Long ago, I got close with my family again. They were shocked when they learned the truth about the Englishman but took me back into the fold with lots of love and forgiveness. Like everyone, I suffer from life's everyday pressures, but my life is mostly good. I successfully steered my life back onto the road of normalcy.

Some years after the divorce, the Englishman called to ask if I wanted to get back together. Imagine my surprise. All I could muster in reply was "You have got to be kidding me." Then, the flood gates opened: "How could you possibly think that I would give up self-development, education, adventure, dating, and freedom to get back with YOU?" It wasn't always easy. Not easy at all. But there was no way I'd let those wild horses hold me back again. Ever. I was and I remain in charge of my own destiny.

In the years following my divorce, I not only achieved my career goals, but I also made up for some of the fun I missed in my teenage years. And I dated a LOT of men—more than I'm comfortable with admitting to. There were fun, fantastic experiences, and many heartbreaking ones, too. In my sampling of the hetero male population, I would have to say that, overall, most are a bit of a disappointment. What's a gal to do?

I have been remarried for a very long time now. Almost 24 years, in fact. I married a tall, lean, blonde from Texas who has great taste in clothes for a straight dude. His big, blue eyes still captivate me. Although his hair has gone gray now, he still looks fantastic in the way that men do as they mature into themselves. Darn them. He's also an attorney, jazz drummer, and dancer.

Is this marriage perfect? Far from it. He's certainly got his flaws and quirks, as do I. A few pieces of the marriage puzzle go missing now and again. They must be found and crammed back in so that the picture stays in focus. A few of the pieces are permanently missing. Like most males, he doesn't care much for the fact that I learn faster, process information more quickly, and know more than he does about many topics. This causes tension. We have the occasional blow out, as a result. But he's not pathologically bi-polar. He's not violent. He's not a control freak. He is decent enough at making and managing money. He is also very generous. He's just an anxious, grumpy drama queen who sees the world as one giant, half-empty glass of water. But he's my family, and he loves me.

He's intelligent, interested in the world, takes me out dancing, makes me laugh, reads to me, rubs my feet, cares for me when I'm ill, does his own laundry, makes the bed, fills up the toilet paper canisters, takes out the trash, and looks after the yard. Well, he watches the guys he pays to look after the yard look after the yard. I hired a housecleaning service. My husband maintains the enlightened idea that the best use of my time is "outside the home." In other words, I'm much more used to our marriage and to society with a career and the ability to earn money. Although he doesn't always "get me," he understands that I must use my gifts and talents to be a fulfilled person. Mostly, he cares for my well-being and works very hard to ensure that we have a safe, lovely, comfortable home. Overall, I can't complain too much—although I do sometimes, like all normal humans, but I honestly don't know what I'd do without him. He's my "snuggle."

Again, I do not wish divorce on anyone. And I still see the purpose of marriage. But women can and should take charge of their own destinies. Every decade, very slowly, women have gained more agency after millennia of oppression. Here is some practical advice: Always keep a job. Always have a bank account of your own. Always keep some savings for escape if it's needed. Keep up relationships with friends and family who could shelter you. Get involved with hobbies, sports, and community groups. Know what government services are available. Always have a plan B. Take time for self-care. And, if divorce becomes necessary, here's a tip. You don't need an expensive lawyer. You don't need a lawyer at all. You can just fill out some forms and file them with the county court. As long as you obtain the signature of your spouse, you're good. You don't need to spend more than the cost of a filing fee. If you have a lot of assets to haggle over, that could be a different situation. But if that's the case, you can probably afford a lawyer. The point is that you can get back on track after a poor decision. It happens. Nobody is perfect. Maybe reading this book will help you. I certainly hope so.

Here are some "fun" facts to end with: My mother died 27 years ago. I miss her every day. My father is still alive as far as I know, but I haven't seen him in 20 years—his choice, not mine. The young woman he married after my mother didn't work out. He moved on to wife #3. My brother died 7 years ago. We eventually grew very close. His wife and his 3 children are dear to me and always will be.

The final big question you likely have is: What of your son? Today, he is married and lives 30 minutes from me. I love him more than anyone on this earth. The Englishman still lives. He is on wife #5. My one consolation is that he has apologized to me more than once.

Lisa Montagne, Ed.D., is a writer, college English professor, and educational technology specialist from Southern California. A former Carnegie Foundation Research Fellow, she has taught English literature and composition at University of California Irvine and Irvine Valley College. Her poetry, creative non-fiction, and fiction have been published by Running Wild Press, World Stage Press, the Arroyo Arts Collective, L.A. Art News Poet's Place, The Ear, The Variant Literature Journal, and others. Red Flags: Tales of Love and Instinct is available from bookshop.org and will be on Audible soon. Montagne also teaches poetry for the Community Literature Initiative, based in Los Angeles. She has been a featured speaker at the Beach City Writers Conference several times and has produced charity and variety shows, including a poetry jam at AWP. Montagne has read her work to audiences in Portland and Tampa, and all over Los Angeles, including at the Beyond Baroque poetry center, at Lummis Day, for the Arroyo Arts Collective, and for Writ Large Press' series Drunken Masters. When she isn't at an open mic night, she is a Swing, Blues and Argentine Tango dancer and DJ who founded the Orange County Blues Collective. See more at lisamontagne.com.

Chapter 3
Septic Love

I grew up in a house with both parents, and I knew I was loved – no matter what. I waited until later in life to get married. In fact, I'd been engaged three times before I actually walked down the aisle. They say *the third time's a charm*. What seemed to be a fairytale turned out to be a complete nightmare. I am intuitive, passionate, introverted, and I care about people. I am kind hearted and also an empath. I had a vision of positivity for my life.

I knew early on that there was something very wrong with my marriage, I just couldn't put my finger on what it was. I had never experienced anything like it! We were supposed to be on the same team, a partnership, but I was made to feel less than. In fact, I might as well have been a turd in the backyard.

My ex and I had a whirlwind romance. We dated for a number of months, moved in, got engaged, and got married. We were older, so there was no reason to drag the time frame out. In the beginning, he doted on me. It felt amazing, like a romantic movie, and who doesn't want a Cinderella story, right? The caring qualities morphed into possessive qualities like crazy accusations of where I was and who I was with. I now realize he was most likely doing all the things he accused me of. I can remember being in big trouble if I was unable to answer his calls. He had four jobs in five years, yet never took responsibility for his choices. It was always someone else's fault. Everything revolved around his perceived lack of respect. I would dismiss things like him buying me an item of clothing that was two sizes too small because I thought it was just human error. Now I know he did it to make a point. He wished I wore that size. He would blindside me. Just when I thought everything was ok, the lull before the storm, out of nowhere he'd suddenly be very angry. I had no idea why or what I'd done. Sometimes he was angry about something that had happened months prior. He ruined every holiday. His behavior gradu ally got worse and worse until I could no longer stand to be around him.

Nothing I experienced in my marriage was like the love described in I Corinthians 13:4-8. It wasn't patient, it wasn't kind; it was arrogant, rude, and self-seeking. It was easily angered; it kept record of all wrongs. It delighted in evil – destroying the ones he was supposed to love and cherish.

My daughter describes emotional abuse as: talking down to you to the point that you believe what you are being told, digging into you knowing what will hurt you. Intentionally trying to break you down. Being told everything is always your fault, no matter what. Manipulating your emotions to the point that you feel nothing. Complete, insidious mind f&*kery.

I didn't go out with friends. I knew it would cause more trouble than it was worth. I was effectively cut off from people. If I was able to venture out, I had to have one, if not both kids in tow. I wasn't allowed to be sick. When I had pneumonia and the doctor ordered bed rest, I still had to drop off and pick up the kids. It wasn't acceptable for me to just "lay around on the couch." He'd later apologize and say he only acted that way because he cared. Talk about kicking someone when they are down.

Although I worked full-time and contributed financially to the household, I was kept in the dark about everything financial in our relationship. I wasn't even included in many of the money decisions that were made. I was made to feel like nothing I did was right, and that I was overly sensitive, selfish, crazy, a burden. I had been convinced that I wasn't able to make good decisions.

I would shop from sale racks at Macy's or Target, and God truly provided when I had an event to go to and needed a nice dress. I was always able to find something for around twenty dollars. He wore Tommy Bahama. I was expected to work full-time and be a stay-at-home mom at the same time. I was expected to do it all. I was yelled at for spending money on the kids. I was once told I had to return products I had purchased to deal with our children's head lice outbreak. My daughter had a head full of hair and by the time we knew she had lice, it was a total infestation. Generations of lice were living on her scalp. I was the one that had to deal with it all – applying the products, combing through the hair to remove the lice, checking for new lice, dealing with all the pillows, bedding, stuffed animals, and missing work because my children couldn't attend school.

I was expected to have a home cooked meal on the table when he walked through the door at night. My kids and I never knew which version of hubby or father was going to walk through the door after work, Jekyll or Hyde. We were fearful of him. I had concerns that if I stood up to him life would be significantly worse for the kids and me. I lived in agony for years. I retreated within myself as a way of coping. If he wanted to have sex, I wasn't allowed to say no, even if the kids were pounding on our bedroom door. I slept with my back toward him, wept silently, and prayed that God would somehow save my kids and me from this. I felt like I was underwater. I was just under the surface and could see the top. I could barely breathe. It was a terrible feeling.

If my husband felt I was showing too much skin, I was told that I disgusted him. When he was angry, he would yell, shake his head, and drive crazily. There are many times I should have asked him to stop the car and let me out. I was accused of throwing myself at other men – even one 80-something-year-old. Basically, I wasn't allowed to be myself.

My employer asked me to go to our LA office to work for a partial week. I really didn't feel like I could leave the kids. I did everything for them, and I wasn't com fortable leaving them alone with him. My husband told me to go because my employer had been good to me. The first night there, we worked late and had dinner around 10 pm. He texted during dinner and I did not answer, so he called, yelled at me, and hung up, not before demanding that I call as soon as I got to my hotel room. He called, just as I was walking into the room, to continue berating me; "was I going out partying or was I there working?" He told me to have "common sense" and said that I had disrespected him. He told me if I wasn't going to wear my wedding ring, it needed to be resized and if I was wearing a different ring, he wanted it back. He didn't speak to me the rest of the time I was in LA.

One time during my pregnancy, he went out to meet his brother for drinks. By 2 am he wasn't home and I was awakened in the middle of the night by the phone. He was in jail. I'd have to pick him up in the morning, and he "hadn't done" what he'd been accused of. I picked him up the next morning and went straight to work. He'd been arrested for soliciting prostitution. It wasn't the first time. He'd done it once before I met him. Of course, he was innocent both times. There really wasn't any discussion about what had happened. He was driving down a street where prostitutes frequent, and he was dying to go to the bathroom. So instead of shitting his pants he chose to pull over in a strip mall where a prostitute had spoken to him, and he'd been arrested. I don't know about you, but I've NEVER been arrested in my life. I know if I had previously been "wrongfully" arrested for soliciting prostitution, I would have shit my pants that evening rather than chance being arrested a second time for the same charge. Again, I had to keep up appearances and act like nothing was wrong. It was not up for discussion even though it cost us a lot of money.

Another big blow came the night my father passed. My father had been my best friend, my biggest cheerleader, my hero. We had the best relationship. He had open heart surgery in his 50's and dealt with heart issues sporadically until he passed. I was used to the routine. I would receive a call from my mom saying that my dad was being transported to the hospital. By the time I arrived at the hospital, they'd done testing, and he was resting comfortably. This time was different. My husband was nowhere to be found when I received the call. I had no clue where he was so I had to take both kids with me to the hospital. I arrived to find out my favorite person in the whole world had passed. Bless the hospital for being so good at explaining death to my children. Because my father had been intubated, when we saw him, he looked like he was laughing. Honestly, a nice way to remember him. After this, I really struggled trying to care for my grieving mom, my two little ones, and a psycho husband, who let me down during my time of deepest need.

The abuse was all so subtle that I didn't know what hit me. All the beat downs definitely took a toll on me. One day I took an online quiz about abusive relationships. The light bulb finally came on, and I read a book that changed my life forever: *Why Does He Do That? Inside the Minds of Angry and Controlling Men,* by Lundy Bancroft. Within the first five pages I wondered if Lundy had met my husband. The men he was describing were exactly like the man I lived with. This book sent me on the journey of learning about abuse.

I am grateful that I was the strongest version of me, physically and mentally, before I met my husband. If I'd known what I was getting into I would have told him to f&^k off. I had been bamboozled into thinking he was this amazing man. After 14 years, I realized I didn't even know who he was. The man I fell in love with never existed. I had to come to terms with how this happened. How did I marry an abusive person and have no clue? Why did I stay so long? This wasn't what I signed up for. I had to wrap my head around the fact that abusive people delight in destroying those they are supposed to love and protect. I had to rediscover and reinvent myself. I didn't even know who I was or what I liked any more. I was numb.

Along the way, someone suggested we go to counseling. I remember the therapist asking – does he need to be kinder, or do you need thicker skin? It was a complete waste of time. If I shared anything in session, it was later held against me. All the while, I had to pretend to the outside world that everything was wonderful. I could have won an academy award. If I'd told anyone he was abusive most people wouldn't have believed me because he, too, was an expert actor. Ugly things only happened behind the closed doors of our home. Some would say it was an anger management problem, but it was controlled in public, so I disagree.

Our relationship was completely exhausting! When we would argue, it would go around and around in circles. There was never any resolution. When he was mad at me, I would get the silent treatment. He would disappear for hours on end and leave his phone at home. He would take his wedding ring off, take down pictures of the two of us, and put them in drawers. I warned my parents not to be surprised if I divorced him one day because I had no intention of living my entire life like this, and I told him the same thing, multiple times. This was probably the point when I knew the writing was on the wall. Living like this was absolute crazy making. After situations like him disappearing took place, he would act like nothing had happened. I usually wasn't ready to move on.

When my kids were little my son was fascinated with fountains. He especially loved the fountains at Fashion Island in Newport Beach. On one particular outing my daughter needed to go to the bathroom, so I took her. While

I was gone, my son fell into one of the fountains. He wasn't hurt, but he was sopping wet and sobbing. His father's reaction was atrocious. He caused a scene by berating my son and he was very rough while trying to remove my son's wet clothes. Have you ever heard about people in emergency situations who are able to lift cars? I felt that feeling of power come over me in this instance. I could have killed my husband. Literally! But I am a rational person, and there's no way I would have gone to jail and missed out on my beautiful children's life.

Someone called the police on him once because we were out with the kids and my daughter was misbehaving. He slapped her on the leg in public. When we arrived home, there was a knock on the door. It was the police coming to investigate the "slap" incident.

Sometimes I would come home from errands and find my kids in tears. Once I arrived home to find both kids in hysterics. My daughter told me that her dad had pulled her brother's hair. When I questioned my ex about this my husband told me my son needed to learn not to be mouthy. I'm not sure how hair pulling helped with that. You could cut the air with a knife when he targeted the kids. My son was frequently told he held the fork wrong, he wasn't sitting correctly at the dining table, the plate wasn't in the middle, or close enough. Once my son got in trouble for eating leftovers without asking.

Once my ex slapped my daughter across the face three times. When I told him he couldn't do that, he asked why. (Um, because you don't want your daughter thinking it's ok for men to hit her.) It got to the point that if I felt he was enraged with them, I would follow him because he was NOT going to hit my children ever again. He would get crazed and lose control.

Another time, my husband took the kids to work with him and they told his coworkers how mean their dad was at home and how mommy cried often. He was furious and wanted me to punish them. But how do you punish a child for telling the truth when you want to teach them to tell the truth? I felt forced to tell them that there were some things you just don't share outside the house. It was confusing to the kids because their father's actions never matched his words, The kids didn't feel they could be truthful with him. If they did tell the truth he was angry about it. He would tell them they were spoiled, ungrateful, and disrespectful. My son, at a very young age said, "Mom, why don't you just divorce him?" or "You'll never leave him."

All of these things led me to grapple with the idea of divorce. I certainly didn't get married so that I could get divorced. I didn't want to get divorced. I wanted happily-ever-after, to grow old with my partner in crime. But that wasn't to be. I had been brought up in a Christian household. What on earth would God think about me getting a divorce? At first I thought I shouldn't leave because of my children. There were some days post-divorce that I wondered if I should have stayed for their sake because if I was there, I could protect them. But I realized I needed to leave because of them. At the time, I didn't even know where to start.

When we moved north, I was accused of taking him away from his family, but I had lived most of my life in southern California. My brother lived in northern California. I visited him once during my marriage, after the birth of our first child. My brother funded the entire trip, and my husband told me that was a hardship for him, so I decided to check out our finances to see what bills we had to pay and how much went to them monthly. As I started looking at the statements, I saw regularly occurring transactions, all originating at the same business. It wasn't clear from the statements what the business was. It turns out he had been going to the strip club once a week for God knows how long. So, while I was unable to spend money on my kids or myself, he was blowing through money satisfying himself at the strip club and massage parlors. Later on, he would tell me it was my fault he'd gone there because I didn't want to have sex with him. "You're damn straight. You sucked the life out of me. I literally had nothing else to give." Learning about his strip club visits was the last straw. I decided that I had to set a date to leave. It was at this point that I told my family and friends what was going on.

I educated myself about the money situation and went to see WEAVE, a local organization that assists abused women. They provided some great tips and helped me to believe I could take my life back again. My brother took me to see an attorney who gave me a plan of action. I'll forever be grateful to my brother and brother-in-law for their financial assistance. If it wasn't for them, I would never have been able to escape.

I knew I couldn't tell the children because I was afraid one of them would tip my husband off about what I was planning. I got my credit re-established, found a place to move into, and started making a list of what I needed to take. We had a garage full of boxes so I started looking through them and marking them so that when move day came we would know exactly what to take. It felt like I was sleeping with the enemy. I was advised to take very few items to make it as painless as possible for my husband. I had to leave while he was at work, a move that was unlike me, but it was the only option I had.

The guys who assisted with my move had previous-ly been incarcerated – extra protection in case my husband came home and started anything. It was the quickest move in history. I left a typewritten note telling my husband I had left and why. When the kids were out of school, my niece picked them up and brought them to our new place. When they arrived, the kids asked "What are you doing here, Mommy? Why are we here?" I explained that I had finally stood up to their father and that we were not going to live like that anymore. We wouldn't have to walk on eggshells and feel uncomfortable in our own home anymore. We were starting a new, peaceful life.

I served my husband with divorce papers the day after I left. I also removed my ring. If you haven't heard about the INFJ door slam, you should look it up. I had made up my mind and there was no turning back. A friend of my brother's told me to strap on my seatbelt for the six-month divorce period. Boy was he right! California, why the hell is there a six month waiting time? I didn't need any additional time to reconsider or think things through. I was done! I was the one who asked for the divorce, and it was a brutal experience. Here I was thinking that in six months I'd be free. Not! It was dragged out. Although I left almost everything in the house, there were still things that needed to be divided. Custody had to be sorted out. My attorney suggested I use the court mediation process for custody. She said if I wasn't happy with the outcome I could request and pay for private mediation. God had his hand in it all. The court mediator met with the two of us together and the children individually. Per the mediator's proposal, custody was cut back from what was previously given to my husband.

He moved in with a new girlfriend. Unsurprisingly, there was no room for the kids to sleep over. When there was a room available, in between girlfriends, only my son would spend the night. There were periods of time my son felt uncomfortable staying the night. Then the guilt started: "I've been alone for two weeks. I deserve sympathy." "I'm not telling you to make you feel bad." Essentially, I had almost 100% custody. I could have taken my ex-husband back to court for more support, but I didn't think it was worth it. I could have requested alimony, but I was afraid he'd quit his job and I'd have to pay him, so I declined that option. When setting the holiday visitation schedule, it didn't include Christmas Eve in addition to Christmas. We had to rotate Christmas Eve and Christmas Day each year. We ended up spending some holidays all together because if we didn't, he wouldn't have seen our daughter because she wouldn't go with him.

I hated being apart from the kids. While it was nice to have some solitude, I was stressed out wondering how they were being treated. And not being with them for holidays sucked.

We had a secret word they could call and say if there were any issues. The secret word was ingenious because it worked in any situation when they felt unsafe and no one on their end would know. One time, my son called, said the safe word, and hung up. I called my ex without letting on that he had called. When the kids came home, they told me my ex had lost it and was screaming at both of them. They were afraid he would hurt them. I spoke to my ex and told him the kids were completely freaked out and did not feel safe due to his behavior. I told him he was an adult and needed to control his emotions because even if he apologized, he couldn't take it back.

I might as well have been a single parent all along. I did everything for them. I just kept trudging forward. I was triggered every time I'd see his name appear on my phone or an email. It was always "what now?"

We were ordered to take a co-parenting class. What a joke to think an abuser can co-parent. In an abuser's mind nothing is done in the best interest of the child. It's all about retaliation for you having left. What I did learn during co-parenting class is that the kids were going to be okay. It was in my best interest for my ex to have a significant other who would love my kids and not to introduce my kids to any boyfriend unless I knew for sure I was going to marry him. Otherwise, it would be like another divorce for the kids to deal with.

My ex didn't get ordered to pay child support right away. I'm glad I put him in the system for child support. Before I did that, he would pick and choose when to give me money. The court ordered him to pay for the kids' medical insurance, half of doctor co-pays, and school expenses. The court's rule requires you to submit receipts within 30 days of the event or expense; the other parent is supposed to reimburse within 15 days, but he didn't. Why does the compliant parent get punished – even if an ex submits receipts late? I was on top of submitting receipts when I first started, but when I didn't receive reimbursements within 15 days, I got lax. I still paid all of the money to cover the kids' needs, even as my ex made considerably more money than I did. There has been no punishment for him not complying with the court order. Regardless, the situation has taught me that it is important to stay on top of submitting receipts within 30 days and keep a running list. It's been over eight years since the child-support order and there's no way my list is complete at this point. A piece of advice, please submit your expense receipts To complicate matters more, my ex was also supposed to pay a percentage of the monthly bonuses he received. This never happened.

The court asks that both parents provide a wardrobe, toys, and personal belongings, so the kids don't have to be inconvenienced taking things back and forth. That never happened and their father would sometimes keep what the kids had taken over. Consequently, I provided what they used at both places. I want to encourage those of you in this situation to take your baby daddy back to court. I was afraid to do so, because court is intimidating and so was my ex, and partly because my kids weren't going to see their dad as often as they were supposed to. I thought I'd get into trouble. It turns out that in California, the court that deals with support and financial issues is not the same court that deals with custody. Looking at the situation now, from the other side, I should have taken my ex back to court for more child support as I had the kids ninety-eight percent of the time for many years. He owes thousands of dollars to me, and there's nothing I can do about it because my kids are now over eighteen.

When I left, I desperately wanted peace. I would make dream boards filled with pictures of things I liked and sayings that spoke to me. I read a lot. I educated myself on abuse and narcissism. I was the stable parent for my kids. My plate was full, and my kids were my priority.

Shortly after I left, my husband started sending me grandiose flower arrangements. They were big enough to decorate an office lobby. Of course, I found out that while he was begging me to return to him, he was on dating sites trying to meet other women. If what I'm about to say isn't a God thing, I'm not sure what it is. It turns out he'd set a date with the single mom who sat right outside my office door at work! Read that again. Of all the I-don't-know-how-many women who live in Sacramento, he'd managed to pick the one that sat right outside my office door. To me, that was confirmation that I had made the right decision to leave.

You may be asking yourself, how are the kids? As soon as I left, I started them in therapy. I felt they needed it to deal with the abuse and separation. My daughter is still in therapy. God has His hand in everything. It was very difficult trying to carry the weight of their feelings and emotions as well as my own. COVID screwed things up – and that made life even more of a "this isn't what I signed up for." My son went from being an "A" student to being an "F" student. This really doesn't work for a child who is highly anxious and a perfectionist. The good news is that he ended up testing out of high school CHSPE (California High School Proficiency Exam) two years early and started at community college. By the time he should have been graduating high school, he had his Associates degree. He is now in his final year of college. He is a go-getter and full of self-confidence, despite the abuse he endured from his father.

My daughter has suffered from anxiety and depression for years. There have been many challenges along the way and she still regularly goes to therapy. COVID affected her too. She did well with the online classes but when schools opened back up she had difficulties due to social anxiety. She missed a lot of school because she "couldn't face" going to school. I have never experienced depression, so I was at a loss of how to handle her situation. I was completely freaked out that we could be in trouble for her "truancy." Thank goodness her high school had a home hospital program that allowed her to stay home and salvage as many classes as possible. During this time, she was attending an intensive outpatient mental health program. I knew that school, as I know it, was no longer an option for her.

I ended up finding an amazing online school for her, California Connections Academy. The learning curve, how classes and attendance worked, and how to turn in work, was a little brutal at first, but it ended up being the best decision we ever made. During her senior year, she was in a special program to help her acquire the credits she needed to graduate. She had the most amazing homeroom teacher who would touch base with her weekly to give her an outline of what she needed to focus on that week. I was part of some of these weekly meetings allowing us all to be on the same page. Honestly, without the help of this institution and her teacher, Mrs. Casillo (I can't say enough about Mrs. Castillo) who had the style my daughter needed and who pointed out truths and also encouraged her, I'm not sure my daughter would have graduated. I am forever indebted to the school and teachers. The school put on a lovely graduation at UC Berkeley for this class of students who had never met each other. I'm still trying to wrap my mind around the fact that 250 kids can graduate and not know anyone else in their class. I'm not sure what my daughter will pursue going forward, but I know the world awaits her talent. I'm extremely proud of both of my children and know they are going to impact the world.

My marriage almost destroyed me but I have found I am strong beyond what I ever thought I could endure. I had to be my own hero. There were some dark days but I remained positive and didn't lose the dream of finding my happily-ever-after. With time, things do get better.

While I wish my ex lived on a different planet, I don't wish him any harm. I can tolerate being in the same room with him, in small doses. He has lost any hold he had over me. He will never scare me again. Now his behavior just reminds me of why I left, and he does not disappoint. My kids are both over eighteen, and he still sends messages that we need to sit and talk to the kids together about this or that. Not going to happen. It never worked before. It's not going to work now.

What always helps me in difficult situations is realizing someone has been through what I'm going through and survived. If they can do it, so can I. While life hasn't been peachy for me, I try my best to focus on positives. My advice is to see the good. If you need to have a pity party, have it, but make it a short one.

I am now at a point where I can say I'm the happiest I've ever been in my life. I have found my peace. I was able to buy a house so we wouldn't have to keep moving around. While the house isn't always spotless (yes, we live here) and the sink is sometimes (well, often) full of dishes, we made it! I am still learning to deal with my trauma and retraining my mind. We survived. If I can inspire even one person with my story, it's a win. It's wonderful to know that our best days are still to come.

RESOURCES

Books

The Five Love Languages, Gary Chapman

Inside the Minds of Angry and Controlling Men: Why Does He Do That?, Lundy Bancroft

Leave a Cheater, Gain a Life: The Chump Lady's Survival Guide, Tracy Schorn

The Christian Chick's Guide to Surviving Divorce, Suzanne Reeves

Healing From Hidden Abuse – A Journey Through the Stages of Recovery from Psychological Abuse, Shannon Thomas, LCSW

Exposing Financial Abuse – When Money is a Weapon, Shannon Thomas, LCSW

Unraveling – Hanging on to Faith Through the End of a Christian Marriage, Elisabeth Klein Corcoran

Rising Strong – How the Ability to Reset Transforms the Way We Live, Love, Parent, and Lead, Brene Brown, PhD., LMSW

The Covert Passive Aggressive Narcissist – Recognizing the Traits and Finding Healing After Hidden Emotional and Psychological Abuse, Debbie Mirza

The High 5 Habit, Mel Robbins

Seeing Beautiful Again: 50 Devotions to find redemption in every part of your story, Lysa Terkeurst

Articles
12 Traits of an Abusive Relationship (Crosswalk.com)
30 Signs of Emotional Abuse (liveboldandbloom.com)
Facebook Groups
You will survive, infidelity support; Beyond Hurt: Women
Thriving After Emotional Abuse; Overcome Narcissistic
Abuse; High 5 Crew with Mel Robbins; Finding Love
and Success After a Toxic Relationship; Emotional Abuse
Awareness and Support; A Place for Us – Sep/Div; One
Mom's Battle, Tina Swithin; Patrick Weaver

Cheap Cell Phone
If your ex is blowing up your phone after you leave, pur-
chase a cheap cell phone and give that number only to those
who need to have contact with you. Put your other phone in
a drawer, and don't check it.

Innocent Spouse-IRS Issues
 If you owe money to the IRS and you have been a victim
of financial abuse in your marriage, look at the Innocent
Spouse form (The IRS appears to know more about emotional abuse than the court system and judges).

Secret Word
Create a secret word with your kids. They can use it in case
they are ever anywhere they feel unsafe and want to be
picked up.

Affirmations
*Keep feeding your mind with positivity. Say affirmations
daily*
Great things always happen to me!
I deserve a loving, healthy relationship.
I deserve a peaceful space to live.
Good morning, beautiful! Good morning, you blessed,

prosperous, successful, strong, talented, creative, confident, secure, disciplined, focused, highly favored child of the Most High God.

I am powerful. I am strong. I am an overcomer. I am a difference maker. I am here to change the world. I am healthy. I am ready to take on any challenge that comes my way. I am more courageous than my fears. Life is tough but I am tougher. I am a warrior.

Play List

Create a custom playlist of music that speaks to you, makes you feel happy, makes you feel strong.

"You Say" Lauren Daigle

"This is my Fight Song" Rachel Platten

"Roar" Katy Perry

"Happy" Pharrell Williams

"Beautiful Day" U2

"I'm Still Standing" Elton John

Ella Estefani resides in northern California with her two young-adult children. She shares her story in the hopes that it will inspire and encourage others in similar situations to take back their lives. She lived for years in an abusive marriage. While she knew something was very wrong early on, she couldn't quite put her finger on what it was (She had never experienced anything like it!) – until she read a book that turned on the lightbulb and changed her life forever. By sharing what she has learned through her own process of discovery, healing, and reinventing herself, she aspires to help you realize that you are stronger than you think, and you deserve true love and happiness. If she can do it, why not you? The road has not been without its bumps, but the journey has been so worth it. In looking back, she knows that God has protected her every step of the way. She couldn't have done any of this without Him or the love, support, and encouragement of her family and close friends. She'd also like to give a shout out to Primerica. Without exposure to their program of self-improvement, positive thinking, changing your mindset, and feeling the fear but doing it anyway, she might not have made it out. May you be blessed.

Chapter 4
From Harmony to Disoonance

Ever since I was a little girl I knew I wanted a family, I wanted to get married and have kids. I always looked up to my parent's relationship. They were high school sweethearts and I thought that was so romantic. I would watch romance movies and fantasize of having my happily ever after. Growing up, my parents took on Mexican traditional roles. Mom took care of all of the children's needs and housework, while dad took on the role of provider. Despite coming to the US with nothing, my parents always made our lives feel as seamless as possible. We were never aware of their struggles. My dad's hard work allowed us to achieve the American dream, while mom always made our home look beautiful. She would even make our clothes so we always looked sharp. Everything looked so seamless and beautiful.

I met my ex-husband in the high school marching band, I was a freshman and he was a sophomore. We met and quickly hit it off. We had so many things in common, from our birthdays to our interests as well as the way we were brought up. It seemed like a match made in heaven. I was naive and all I knew was that I wanted to marry my high school sweetheart, have kids, and live happily ever after.

While in college, I married my high school sweetheart, my dream came true. After completing college I had my first child. A year later I had my second child. Both my husband and I decided to take on traditional roles, just like my parents. I became a stay at home mom and my ex-husband was the provider. I would go to my doctor appointments by myself as he was working to provide for us. After my children were delivered, my husband wanted privacy. He made it clear that he didn't want my mom or his mom to be at our home to help me with our boys. Once we got home from the hospital I was on my own. I thought the saying was "it takes a village to raise kids" in this case, the village was a party of one, me. I thought I had to be ok with doing things alone because my partner was out making the money. My responsibility was to take care of the kids and our home. My mom did it, and it seemed so smooth. I asked myself "Why am I having a hard time?"

Before having kids I was a woman with a career, a go-getter, I had a social life. All of a sudden I became a stay at home mom. My previous life was non-existent. My career was placed on hold, my social life became minimal. I had little to no sleep, no one to talk to about my real feelings, and my mental health was suffering. All of my time was now dedicated to two babies who needed my every second. My children were fifteen months apart which made everything much harder. While having all of these feelings I had to keep up with "being a good wife." I was expected to keep a clean home, cook, clean, do laundry and run errands. I became a different person. I felt so much sadness and anxiety. I felt so alone and abandoned. Many times I found myself in my room crying with my babies by my side. I didn't realize I had postpartum depression. I didn't want to express any weakness because of my fear of being judged. I found life extremely difficult, being the people pleaser that I am, I didn't speak up. Not wanting to make anyone upset, I would try my best to figure things out on my own. I wanted a drama free home but I was pushing myself to the limit.

I began to grow resentful toward my husband. I was sad and disappointed with life. I thought that what I was living and feeling was part of the transition to having kids. I thought my feelings were normal. Isn't this what my parents did? I thought I was being weak, so I pushed through it and rolled with the punches. I didn't think marriage was supposed to make me feel this lonely. The resentment became stronger in my relationship, we were both so young, but we were doing our best. We didn't go to marriage counseling. We didn't have the right tools to help us navigate through being married and raising children together.

As life went on I realized my husband and I didn't have the same interests. As a people person, my weekends were usually filled with lots of activities involving big crowds and lots of friends. He, on the other hand, was more of a homebody. He was not comfortable being in large crowds. So many of the things I liked, he didn't. Weekends with my husband were spent doing things he enjoyed. I later grew to love them too. Our different personalities made it hard because we spent most of our time doing things he enjoyed which added to my feelings of resentment.

I believed in marriage being forever, but I had one deal breaker. At year eighteen of our relationship, my life changed very suddenly, we went through a hardship that turned my deal breaker into our reality. We tried couples counseling. I found it very hard to forgive, but I gave our relationship my all. We tried to make it work for six months, but things didn't work out. It became too painful for me to stay in the relationship.

In a relationship both parties have to work together to make things work. Our shortcomings were a by-product of the divorce. My lack of communication to express my needs and not having the right tools to know how to navigate through marriage made it hard to keep our marriage together. I learned that we were both unhappy, but both of us failed at communicating our needs to each other.

I tend to be an organized person and I like to follow rules. Thus far, I had followed every rule in the society norms rule book. I got a degree, got married, had babies, and bought a home. I was supposed to live happily ever after. Isn't that how it's supposed to go? I see my life as a file cabinet that is neatly organized. Every life event gets neatly stored in a beautiful cabinet labeled "Lily's Life." Before the divorce I thought my life was organized. After the divorce it was as though my precious file cabinet had been drug through swampy lands. All of a sudden the cabinet tipped over and files were all over the swamp. The most important and precious files I cared most about, those of my marriage, were being devoured by a vicious horrifying monster called divorce. I saw myself trying to save the files that meant so much to me but there was no way of saving them. Grieving, with a heavy heart, I looked at the mess of papers and files, dirty and bent, and I felt overwhelmed. Is it even possible to put this plethora of important papers back into what were once neatly organized files? The cabinet would never be the same. Never complete, with a purpose or ability to attain the file labeled "lives happily ever after."

All of the feelings I felt were so intense. The grief was like a shot of potent poison which ran through my veins in immense sorrow and pain, day in and day out. There was no escaping it. Not knowing if it would ever go away, I became desperate. This pain was taking a toll on my physical health. I remember crying everywhere I went. The dark cloud followed me everywhere. Despite feeling such sadness and emptiness, I carried on with normal life in the hopes of making life as normal as possible for my boys. I tried everything to make myself happy. The things that used to bring me joy had no effect. At one point I had intrusive thoughts. What if I end my life? The pain was too strong I couldn't take it anymore, but the thought of having my kids live knowing that their mom committed suicide was too much to bear. I thought of the sadness my death would bring my family and friends.

After the divorce I felt a large void in my life and in my soul. My heart was shattered into a million little pieces. I felt as if I had been kicked out of my safe place. I felt homeless and abandoned. I no longer had the man I thought was my life long partner. I was full of so many emotions and had no idea how to deal with them. My close friends had my back, and were ready to take off their hoops to fight for me, but they didn't understand the hurt I was going through because no one in my family or friends had ever been divorced. I had so many questions, so many feelings. Divorce was not a file in my cabinet. I wished there was a handbook to tell me how I could organize this mess of a life I was experiencing. Some people would say "Why do you feel this way for a man?" and "There are many fish in the sea." The person closest to me would say "Why can't you just get over it?" I didn't feel understood.

I was afraid of the unknown and all of the insecurities. I would ask myself so many questions. Where will I end up? How will I be able to take care of my children financially and still take care of our home? How do I navigate being a single mom? Who would ever want to be with me? Am I not beautiful enough? Am I not smart enough? Does love really exist? Why did this happen to me? Why was I not enough? What did I do to deserve this? Who would ever love me for who I am? Who would ever love my kids as their own? Will I ever be happy again? Can I ever trust men? I felt like a failure. These feelings took me back to my childhood and I thought of myself as a dumb little Mexican girl. I thought I didn't deserve love because I was not smart enough or beautiful enough. I thought I would end up alone.

After the divorce, I didn't believe in love anymore. I remember seeing couples holding hands and thinking it was all a lie. Love was just something someone made up for lame romance movies, to make you feel all warm and fuzzy. I remember having nightmares, which happened often. I would wake up shaking, crying uncontrollably, and covered in sweat. Most of them had to do with demons, large yellow snakes, and people trying to hurt me. I didn't have happiness, a dark cloud followed me everywhere. In real life. In my sleep. I felt like a victim, stripped of everything good. The only good thing left were my boys.

Despite all of the sorrow and pain, I would always think about my sweet innocent boys. They gave me the strength to get up in the morning and push through my day.

My boys were my everything and I was going to fight to give them the best life possible. I came to the conclusion that wanting to end my life was selfish. My kids need me. My goal was not to allow them to feel like their life was missing anything. I always reminded them to see the good in things. I reminded them that they get to celebrate everything twice and get double the presents. Double the love.

After the break-up with my ex-husband, at the age of thirty-four, I decided to make a career change and get my teaching credential. This would allow me to have the same schedule as my boys. I had to take state exams, but I had a hard time passing them because I was in a deep depression. I wasn't going to let depression stop me from being the mom my kids deserved. My kids saw me cry everytime I failed an exam but they also saw me jump with joy and happy tears when I did pass. They were witness to struggle and perseverance. I'm grateful that they got to witness my struggles because I wanted them to learn that life can be hard. I wanted them to learn to keep fighting for what you want. They know I could have gone back into architecture or real estate but I decided to become a teacher for them.

Following the divorce I went out into the uncharted territory of the dating world, something I had not done in nineteen years. It all became really complicated. I had to learn the difference between seeing each other, hooking up, situationship, boyfriend, girlfriend, and more. What happened to just being boyfriend and girlfriend? I had no clue how to navigate this new world but I knew I didn't want to be alone.

I dove into dating without being educated on the subject. I dated unintentionally. I wasn't clear on my values, what I was looking for, what I wanted, what my deal breakers were, or what was important to me. I filled my loneliness with dating and I failed many times. I was giving up on men. After many dates I began to think that all men were cheaters, liars, and were self-centered with no goals or aspirations. Dating in my late thirties with kids and finding prince charming appeared beyond my reach. Being the people pleaser that I am made things more complicated. I gave men the benefit of the doubt and gave them more chances than I should have. I was hopeful that they could be the man I imagined they were. I realized that being vulnerable and opening my heart to the wrong men was causing me too much pain.

From the beginning of my dating journey I knew that I didn't want to have any more children. I also knew that I wanted to make sure I always took my kids into consideration. I didn't want my children to meet any man I didn't see a future with. The man I brought home would have to be a good example for my kids and if that man had kids, those kids would have to be a good influence for my boys. Dating someone was not just about my needs and wants. I made sure I thought of my boys in this equation.

I decided I was no longer going to dwell in the past but instead, use the past to my advantage. I decided to learn from every relationship, assess what I liked and didn't like, consider how these men made me feel and why. Doing this helped me learn more about myself. I started better understanding what kind of relationship I wanted. I knew I didn't want to go through another divorce so I had to educate myself. I knew that relationships can't be perfect. Relationships have disagreements and arguments. The important thing was knowing how to handle them. A relationship is about mutual respect, understanding, empathy, communication, clarity, vulnerability, respecting, boundaries, and lifting each other up. I still find myself feeling lonely even though my kids are very present in my life. I find that humans need that physical connection from that special kind of love. We need to feel loved and wanted and to know that the right man will come at the right time.

In dating, I struggle with people pleasing and not seeing my worth. Through the years I have worked on healing myself and learning how to have a good relationship not only with myself, but with everyone around me. I had a conversation with my relationship coach and she pointed out that I have a hard time trusting myself to make the right decision. She said I need to learn to trust my gut and not seek reassurance from others, that my feelings are valid. She also said that I am doing really well with my journey, with setting clear boundaries, and with picking myself first. Hearing this from a professional really helped boost my self esteem. I now realize that all the hard work I have put into this journey is evident. I know that I need to keep showing up for myself, the same as I wish my person would show up for me. I need to keep using the tools I've learned and put them into practice. I am more intentional with dating and I don't give any man a chance just because they show interest and say they love me. I have a better idea of what to look for and what I need. I am more clear on knowing my deal breakers and I am more confident in my dating skills.

It is now year seven since the divorce. All the chaos of the divorce has now settled. The days filled with rivers of tears, the thoughts of not knowing what my future holds, and the terrifying nightmares are gone. All of the nights thinking I wasn't enough, and that I was not worthy of being loved have vanished. The insecurity of not knowing if I can support my household on my own has diminished. The arguments with my ex-husband are obsolete.

Right after the divorce I joined Divorce Care through a local church. It was great and my kids were able to benefit from it too. Before taking the course I felt like my feelings weren't valid. I couldn't understand why I couldn't just "get over it" as I was once told. I thought there was something wrong with me for being so heart broken. We watched a video in class that mentioned that divorce can feel like you want to drive off a cliff. It can feel like you lost the person you love the most, a person who is still alive and giving that love to someone else. When I realized I was not crazy, I finally felt understood.

About two years after the divorce I sought therapy. My therapist suggested I read *Do Yourself a Favor… Forgive,* by Joice Meyer. I made a decision to forgive my ex-husband, not for his sake, but for my happiness. Forgiving someone is a choice. Being upset at him made me bitter and sad, not allowing me to enjoy the beauty of life. I didn't want anger to take up real estate in my mind and in my heart. Today we have a civil relationship. We respect each other's relationships and want nothing but the best for one another. I believe that his happiness will allow him to be the happy loving father that my children deserve. If I'm happy I will also be able to show up as a better mom. It is important to admit that we are human. No one is perfect, we all make mistakes and are flawed, including me. Forgiving and forgetting are two different things. I chose to forgive.

After a recent breakup, a friend reached out to me and invited me to a church group called Positively Engaging Women. I was sad and down on myself, I was tempted to reject her invitation, I am so glad that I accepted. I made new friends and learned so much. After listening to my story a group member suggested I join a Step Study group through another church. Again, I am so glad I joined because I made more friends and was able to pour out all of my pain, hang-ups, and habits. I was able to reflect on my life and what I had to work on in order to achieve my goal of living a happier life. I have learned that even when I don't feel like doing something, pushing myself to do it can end up being the best decision. Pushing myself helped me get out of my funk.

"Take this time to find yourself" is what I heard from others. What does finding yourself mean? I found myself confused but as I began to learn to love myself I learned who I was without being defined as a husband-wife unit. I became my own individual, beautiful unit as a single mom. I learned to embrace my singleness, and not see being single as a bad thing. I learned what I enjoyed doing and what I wanted in life. I found that the person we spend the most time with is ourselves, and learned to love my own company. I learned to date myself and take care of myself. By doing these things, you too can learn who you are and what you need. This can look like going on solo dates, pampering yourself, looking at yourself in the mirror and giving yourself compliments. "Dang girl, you look fine!" Also, if something doesn't go as planned, or you make mistakes, remember to be kind to yourself. Be proud of yourself for all of your accomplishments, even the small ones. Give yourself love as if you were your own best friend. Learn to romanticize your life, do things that would help make your life feel magical. It might mean you light a candle and play pleasant music while cooking. Or it can look like basking in the sun with a fancy coffee in a special mug. Or picking up your favorite meal and having a picnic while enjoying the beauty of nature. Or picking up flowers for yourself.

I came to the realization that there would be times when I would look at myself in the mirror and point out all of the things I was insecure about. I learned to shift my thoughts, especially when I was feeling down on myself. When I didn't feel my best, I put extra effort into making myself look good, because when I look good, I feel good. If you are going through a rough patch remember, this too shall pass, there's always a rainbow after the storm. Don't wait for the big job, the big house, the perfect relationship to be happy. Be grateful for what you have now, at this moment. There are people who wish they had what you have. Maybe you might not have your person yet, but enjoy your single self. This chapter of your life can also be beautiful

I enjoy journaling and I like to be intentional. I make a point to write at least three things I am grateful for, what I am proud of myself for, why I love being me, and anything that happened in my day. After the divorce I decided I was going to create a bucket list and experience as many things on the list as I could. I went to my first concert at the age of thirty-five. If a friend invites me to something new, even if it's not my thing, I will try it. My only rules are "Don't get me in trouble" and "Don't get me killed." You never know what you like unless you try. This mentality has allowed me to experience so many fun things, and have unforgettable experiences. I can even say I have run a half marathon. Don't be afraid to try things on your own. Life is too short!

"Tap into your femininity" is another thing that people would also say to me. What in the world does this mean? After my most recent breakup, I decided to join a Salsa class and I learned so much. The class helped me gain confidence and tap into my sensuality. I have never been a dancer because I thought I had two left feet. It turns out I have a left and a right foot and I do a pretty good job at using them. While dancing I would constantly be reminded that I had to allow my partner to lead, my argument was "I'm an independent woman." I am learning that I have to trust myself and the right partner in order to dance in sync and create a beautiful dance. Just like in a relationship, I have to trust myself and my partner to dance in tandem. In order to create the beautiful dance of marriage both partners must want to dance the same dance. Both partners must put in the work. A relationship, a marriage, takes constant work, constant growth, constant lead and follow, compromise, and lots of trust.

I have also learned that I can't change another person regardless of the situation. In dating, I have learned that I can only change my own actions. If I set boundaries and a person or people don't respect my boundaries, the only thing I can do is voice my concern. If they still don't take my feelings into consideration, the best choice is to choose myself and leave that relationship. Be a little selfish. Choose your happiness and mental well being first.

I have also come to the realization that people get older and often grow into different people. Pause and think about it. Are you the same person you were ten years ago? Most likely not. You may have different interests, values, fashion choices, aspirations, needs and wants. I am definitely not the same person I was ten years ago. Dating has given me a better idea of what my love language is and what I need to be happy in a relationship. I take every experience as an opportunity to learn and grow. Every romantic relationship, or friendship whether good or bad will always teach you something new about yourself and about others. It is key not to let a bad situation permanently define your life. It is okay to have feelings about bad situations. Don't stay with those feelings for the rest of your life. Many times we have to go to hell and back to come up on top, to grow, and to become a better version of ourselves.

Events and people in our life help shape us into who we are today. They help us learn about who we are and what we want. Sometimes events have a good impact and sometimes they don't. The difference is how we allow these things to affect us moving forward in life. Learning from experiences can help us see life in a different light and make us feel grateful for the things we have. Learning can also help us understand that things are happening for us, not to us. Life is rarely perfect. We share a world with humans who also have a story, who also experience struggles. We have all been hurt, and unfortunately many times hurt people hurt people. Sadly, because of bad events in our lives, we grow insecurities we didn't know we had. We have to unlearn negative thoughts and behaviors. We all have a choice to be a better version of ourselves. Otherwise we chose to stay the same and allow sorrow to take over our lives. Placing blame on everyone else for our struggles will slowly kill our joy. We can create the life we want, help ourselves, by seeking help from a professional, reading books, listening to podcasts, joining a group, or going to church. Remember, no one will help you if you don't want to be helped. You have to want to be helped. Life is about choices.

I, like most people, am afraid of change, the unknown, and the "what if's" of life. I have learned that I can't plan my life neatly in a file cabinet the way I had imagined. At some point I had to let go and go with the flow of life. Creating an inventory with a set of tools has helped me navigate through the storms of life. Tools are essential. Knowing how to deal with the hurts and hang-ups of life is important. Knowing your own worth and how to love yourself is important above all.

I know now that I am beautiful just the way I am, I am smart, loving, and caring. I am a great mom, friend, daughter, and amazing teacher. I am worthy of being loved, and I can be a magnificent girlfriend and wife. I choose not to be a victim of my past. My past doesn't define me. Notice I call it "the divorce" not "my divorce." My past has helped mold me into the beautiful person I have become. I may not have a prince charming by my side, but I have found myself and now I have joy. I have learned to enjoy life and romanticize my own life. I am grateful for what I have. I have created a beautiful home for my kids and for myself. I hang out with friends and family and do the things I love. I know I am not perfect, and I will have sad days, but I always aim to be a better version of myself each day. If someone doesn't choose me, I let them. Mel Robbins says in her book, *The Power of Let Them,* not to worry about the things I can't control. It can be hard, but I am trying my best. I know the importance of setting boundaries and I am learning to better express my feelings without hurting others. If people can't respect my boundaries, then I respectfully take myself out of the equation, I "let them." I carry on with my life. I cry. I allow myself to experience all of the feelings, but I don't let feelings pull me down. I love and embrace my chapter of being a single mom. If someone comes into my life and adds to my happiness, helps make me a better version of myself, that's where the money is at. I am not settling for someone just because they say they love me. I do know there is someone out there meant for me, the right time will come. I am having fun and showing up for myself while I wait.

Divorce has been the best decision within which I have found myself and learned to love my life. The divorce has helped make my boys responsible and grateful young men as they learn teamwork in our household and how to be there for one another. They have witnessed a healthy co-parenting relationship. The divorce journey has helped me learn that I am not a dumb little Mexican girl. I am a smart, beautiful, fierce Mexican woman who is worthy of love.

*

Do Yourself a Favor... Forgive by Joice Meyer
The Let Them Theory by Mel Robbins
8 Rules of Love by Jay Shetty
Divorce Care
Celebrate Recovery Group
Relationship coaches
Therapy

Lily Oropeza was born in Mexico. Leaving her extended family, her parents decided to immigrate to the United States when she was three years old. She was raised in East Los Angeles, and didn't learn English until fifth grade. Despite attending a school with mostly Latinos, she quickly realized that not knowing the language and having an accent would make her the target of teasing, and she feared becoming the laughing stock of her class. She learned to blend in by being a people pleaser and saw herself as the dumb little Mexican girl who couldn't speak English. While not feeling enough, she worked hard on this new language, and worked on her accent in order to fit in.

In her adult years she got a BA in Architecture. While in school at the age of twenty two she married her high school sweetheart. Shortly after she had her two beautiful boys. She became a stay at home mom, but given that she is a goal getter she became a realtor. At the age of 34 her world came crumbling down, she got divorced and had to say goodbye to what she had fantasized to be her forever partner. Quickly she went back to school and got her multiple subject teaching credential and Masters in education.

Lily hopes that by sharing her story she can help someone who is going through divorce by providing them with hope and courage. To learn to see their worth and come out of this stronger and happier.

Chapter 5
Never the Right Time

"It is baby steps and giant steps
and tears and laughter
the world seems to take you
in its arms and carry you
until you are strong enough
to run on your own…"

These are a few lines to a poem I wrote about growing. It just seemed to apply in regards to the end of an established relationship and what that entails. When children are involved (regardless of their age) the process takes on another life. The disappointment spreads and someone has to take the blame. The reality that people sometimes grow apart isn't given voice because years of success in perceived love invalidate that option. Though many reasons lead to the dissolving of a relationship, emotions can sometimes cloud clear thought and from the murk and mire emerges an indisputable wrong and the given credence of what is believed. Sides are taken and the beauty of past interaction dies in shallow graves of regret and forgetfulness. Anger has little patience with differences of opinions. Someone is wrong, someone is right. But relationships, like most things in life, are not just black and white, there are mounds and mounds of gray.

For anything to make sense its dawn, birth, inception, conception, origination, genesis, emergence, if possible, must be understood, or at least given some semblance of respect in regards to the overall outcome. So, the beginning is where I will begin. The earliest memories that I have only include me, my mother and a small black dog with a white chest. I do not remember my younger brother and sister (who were twins) or the man who I believed was my father. They all faded into the picture once we all moved into a small house on Hayes avenue in Long Beach. Though spotted at times this is my earliest recollection of what I deemed a family. It was my only reference point and thus my world. Our first night at our new home is my first memory of my father, brother and sister. They seemed to float into my consciousness from out of nowhere. I know they were there prior to the move but for whatever reason I've never been able to pull them up any earlier than this. What I do remember is a haunting fear of my father emerging around this time. I didn't feel connected to my family. There was something about me that felt oddly out of place. I was too young to name or define it, but I could feel it. It was attached to every interaction with the adults that made up my environment. Unsaid but surrounding me like a mist. As I grew the chasm between us only grew wider. Beatings from my father increased, but far more debilitating were the words directed at me. I could endure the belts and back-hands and extension cords but the mean words cut through me like a knife through warm butter. I had no defense for them because they were coming from my father, the man I most admired.

Everything intensified as the years passed but there was one incident that would change my outlook on family, the moment in time where I came to realize that family was who 'treated' you like family. This moment of clarity came when I was eleven years old. I was in the sixth grade and my brother was in the fourth. It was recess time and my brother came to me crying and screaming that some kid was bothering him. I told him to calm down and show me the kid. When he did I was surprised because the boy he pointed to was a good friend of mine and a nice kid. I knew it had just been a misunderstanding so I walked up to the kid (Torey was his name) and asked him what had happened. He was very apologetic and began telling his side of the story. As he's talking my brother comes from the side and socks him right in the eye. Torey goes down crying and holding his eye. I say to my brother, "What are you doing? He was sorry." A crowd gathers and soon a teacher grabs me sternly by my arm. I'm trying to explain that I didn't hit the kid, my brother did. In the office my story is finally listened to. My parents are called anyway. When I get home my mother asks me what happened. I tell her what happened, with my brother present. Later, when my father gets home I have to tell the story again. Everyone now knows that I did not hit the kid. My teacher, Mr. Parker, wants a parent to come so they can talk about 'my' consequences. My father decided to come. I tell my story again and Mr. Parker realizes the consequences (writing 100 times "I will not hit my class-mates") should be my brother's, not mine. My father is quiet for a moment, then says, "Let Jeff write them anyway." My teacher looks confused and I can't believe what I'm hearing. Mr. Parker, speaking in almost a whisper, says, "Mr. Turner, Jeffery didn't do anything wrong."

"I know, but let him write them." I wrote them. At that time I had no idea that Chris Turner wasn't my biological father, but that day something in me died for him and it would only die more in ensuing years. As time passed, a constant promise that I made to myself was, if I ever had kids I would never treat them the way I had been treated. Life had a lot more ass whippings to give me but this promise to myself I would keep no matter what.

People talk about when you survive things it makes you stronger, and I agree. But you lose certain things too. Losing faith in those given the responsibility of taking care of me so young gave me trust issues that bled over into any interactions I had. Feeling as though I didn't belong. I would not allow any children I brought into this world to question if love was in their living space. Early on I knew if I ever became a father, I would be a good one. I simply want-ed to be the opposite of what I had experienced. I was told I'd never amount to anything. But in the back of my young mind I reasoned that, if I was already something (living) that I didn't have to amount to what I already was. But the words still stung. And after certain things had finally come to light I wondered if my biological father had been there to protect me, could that have made a difference?

I decided to marry at nineteen. I was going to marry the first girl who had said she loved me. No experience, no worries. I was proud to sign and pay for our marriage certificate. The future seemed bright because I had nothing to base it on. I was a kid trying to get out of the home that had always treated me like an accident. I would create my own home. And it would grow without beatings or harsh words. My children, if I had any, would be surrounded by so much love that questions of doubt would be nonexistent. There would be no accidents. My family would have a purpose. I was optimistic about a future I had no idea about. It was my fairytale. I would be the father I never had. I wouldn't curse at my children. I wouldn't beat my children. But mostly, I would never destroy their confidence with my words. I ran away from all of that into the arms of my new wife. Hindsight, it wasn't fair to bring all of my issues to this union, but I did, and so did she. The battle had begun, and neither of us had an inkling of what was coming. We believed love would harness its strength and help us in the face of any and everything. Naiveté.

I never said a word to my (step)father about my upcoming wedding. Not a single word (I hated him so much by then) and one day he asked me, "When were you going to tell me about you getting married?" I just replied, "I thought mom would tell you." End of discussion. I was jumping into my future and didn't need his blessings. Right before we were married doctors had told my wife-to-be that she would never be able to have children. We refused to believe that and never shared that news with anyone. Nobody's words were going to stagnate us. She got pregnant and we decided to head to New York where I thought the grass would be greener. It wasn't. Living with my wife's family was probably one of the biggest mistakes I made because it slowly began to eat away at me and our relationship. It seemed as though one challenge after another rose to face us. Just entering our twenties and already life was proving so difficult. When our son was born he didn't want to breathe. Was I cursed? "Breathe!" When he finally did I thanked a god I hadn't spoken to in years. Too many prayers unanswered in my childhood but restoring a heartbeat was beyond my capabilities. Now we had a beautiful baby boy, who cried a lot, but he was breathing. The world felt as though it was holding a grudge against us and sometimes we took it out on one another. We were young dreamers. I was going to sing, and she, dance and act. We ignored the cold, lifeless attic that was our home. Ignored mean in-laws who had invited us to New York only to ostracize us once we arrived. Her family proved no better than mine. I was right, no one could be trusted.

In those first couple of years my son kept me alive. My only inspiration to face each day was him. I loved my wife but I no longer wanted to sing or write or breathe. But the promise I had made to myself about the father I had never had echoed loud in my mind whenever I wanted to end this collision called my life. As tired as I was of dealing with unfulfilled dreams (like everyone else) that promise stood before me like a flashlight that wouldn't go out, a constant reminder. I would leave, wander the streets and then come back. No one had sat me down and talked to me about manhood or fatherhood. I was learning while in the whirlwind. My teachers were harsh realities and my inspiration was a baby everyone said looked like me. I had to figure it out. We had to figure it out. No one was coming to save us because we had nice smiles. Life didn't work that way. We took our frustrations out on each other, not physically but with mean, hurtful words. We weren't really mad at each other, we were mad at the hand dealt us. We deserved better, easier. But we were made resilient instead. Diamonds. After a while I learned to die silently on the inside. There was no complaining, I didn't rage against the system or my family or my past, I raged against myself for losing that childlike curiosity about life. I was twenty-one or twenty-two and already tired. I had always been a big dreamer, and now the dreams were reduced just making it through the week. I found that pretending for an extended amount of time was no longer pretending you became that caricature of yourself, a self that after a while you didn't recognize. Pretending extinguished the fires of passion. Survival was the foreplay and led to long sessions of silence trying to come up with something to say that would bring our forced smiles to an end. A remedy for the resentment that needing too much and having too little brought. We knew the odds were against us but we held each other that much tighter, but the match soiled with disappointment would not ignite. I left a hundred times in my head but my body stayed true to the promise of being a present and loving father.

By the time our daughter was born we had weathered so many storms. Where we got the strength I cannot say, but we came through smiling every time. Everyone thought we had the most solid marriage but at some point I knew I was there for my children and maybe their mother felt the same (though she never said as much). The difficulties had drained our conversations. If we were not talking about our children or the bills our conversation lulled. Life had made us soldiers but at the price of our intimacy. After twenty-six years I walked away. I was the villain to most. But I knew I had tried my best, we both had. She was willing to endure the silence, I wasn't. There is never a good time to walk away from something or someone you have invested so much time in. I was still that damaged little boy who needed fixing. My wife couldn't fix me, no one could. I had to find myself and forgive what needed forgiving and transform what needed changing. And in the end my ex was my biggest supporter and my best friend. She passed away in 2023 after a long battle with cancer. It still doesn't seem fair. This life constantly asked her to fight when all she really wanted to do was love.

When all is said and done there is no easy way to end something you believed had forever attached to it. Being in love does not prepare you for the possibility of one day not being in love. And when children are involved (regardless of their age) it causes a fracture that mends but is always there. What helps is not completely cutting off the communication. Though hard at first, time eases the awkwardness and anger no longer short circuits cordial conversation. It is difficult but not impossible to gain a friend in the throes of losing a lover.

Jeffery Martin is the author of 13 books and contributor to 7 poetry anthologies. His first book Weapon of Choice won best book of poetry in 2008 New Jersey Beach Book Festival. Several of his books have received "honorable mention" in various book contests. Having recently collaborated on a film script, he plans to submit it to various contests. In November 2019, he interviewed professor/activist Noam Chomsky and from that wrote a book of poetry entitled: Muse Moments: Poetry Inspired by Noam Chomsky. Mr. Martin also has a podcast called Write a Way Podcast, where he and his guests discuss writing, the arts and life experiences. He is currently interviewing poets and graffiti artists in hopes of creating a documentary highlighting the power of art and poetry. He resides in California, but considers himself a citizen of the world.

Chapter 6
Run, Don't Walk

From the very first moment I held him in my arms, I knew. I knew I did not want to raise this child of mine with or anywhere near the ex's family. I felt an inexplicable dread, an urgent need to grab my son and run. I couldn't exactly understand the gut feeling that permeated every single living cell. I had no idea, back then, that my spirit guides were sending me a critical warning of imminent danger.

Before I begin this story, I'd like to pose a question or two. Do you believe in evil? Do you believe that there are evil people in this world who will go to any length to try to destroy you and the ones you love? Well this, my friends, is a true tale about love, hate, and pure evil. This is the kind of story that many will find incredulous as it dabbles into other dimensions, those inexplicable to the rational human mind. Consider yourself forewarned.

In the Beginning

He had never mentioned his mother, not until the day we decided to relocate to Mexico and move in with that woman. We had only lived there a month and it was evident that she couldn't stand me, and not because I was a "pocha" or because I didn't know how to cook and had burnt her favorite pot, no. She hated me for the simple fact that I had married her son; that is it, and that is all. Just so that you get a better feel for what kind of person this woman is, her family motto was, and probably still is, as follows (loosely translated, of course), "I made my sons handsome so that they would be financially supported, and made my daughter a "pendeja" so she could be the financial supporter." Well, to her dismay, I hadn't been raised to be anyone's "pendeja!"

Fast Forward 2 ½ Years

I could have died in a Mexican hospital one crisp November morning. I was at my regular, eight-month, prenatal appointment when my primary doctor told me that my blood pressure was through the roof and I needed to check myself into the hospital immediately. As I think back, I question many things. Why was I driving myself to the hospital? Why wasn't the ex with me? The very same questions were asked by the medical staff as well.
At the hospital, I was placed in a room of my own, away from all of the noise, but that didn't last long. Before the night was over a young mother and her newborn were placed by my side. It must have been a curse! That wretched child never stopped crying which meant that the chances of lowering my blood pressure had gone from zero to none. The following day, I was discharged with a diagnosis: preclampsia. The doctors sent me home on full bed-rest orders. The next day, my brothers drove out to Mexico to "rescue me." Not 24 hours after I arrived in California and applied for emergency Medi-Cal, I ended up in Fullerton Hospital's Emergency Room. It turned out that the excruciating abdominal pain that sent me to the ER was my liver at the brink of eruption.

I came to find out, years later, that I didn't just have pre-clampsia. I had actually been diagnosed with HELLP syndrome, a serious, rare pregnancy complication where red blood cells breakdown and liver enzymes are elevated causing low platelet counts. Throughout my entire pregnancy I had been working both night and day without a care in the world. Suddenly, in my last trimester, I could've ended up in a coma, or even worse, dead. Not a single doctor on either side of the fuckin' border had ever mentioned the HELLP diagnosis. It wasn't until I read through my entire medical file, many, many years later, that I discovered the diagnosis that had never been mentioned, written down in my chart all along.

To make matters worse, the doctor from Fullerton managed to elevate my blood pressure even more by reprimanding me for having traveled in my condition. Hello? The reason I had traveled was precisely because of high blood pressure. The doctors in Mexico basically left me to die by sticking a wailing child in my room and then by sending me home. Who in their right mind would release a pregnant patient when their blood pressure was still miles high?

Within a few hours of arrival at Fullerton, I had been moved from the ER to the maternity ward. Labor was induced and my son was born. There we were, my son and I, all alone in the hospital because the ex had no papers to join us. Thankfully, despite having been born a month early, and with all of my complications, my son had no serious health conditions and quickly grew into a plump and happy baby.

After a month, it was time, we went back home to Mexico back to a house where three working adults had spent my maternity check and hadn't paid the rent or the utility bills. I don't think I will ever get answers as to what happened to all of the maternity money. Perhaps the brother-in-law drank it all away. Perhaps the cousin had gone on a shopping spree for her own baby. Or perhaps, it was the ex who had spent all of his lunch hours betting on how many tacos he could down in ten minutes. Yep, that is what my son and I had come home to. This isn't even the worst part of this story. Imagine that!

Shortly after moving back to Mexico, after much insistence, the ex finally agreed to move back to Orange County. I simply refused to be, or allow my son to be, anywhere near his family. Even though it had been his choice to jump over the border and cross the desert on foot, he had managed to turn himself into the victim and convinced my parents, my whole family, that I was the bad person. The whole time we were in Mexico, he could have sacrificed his Saturday mornings to do his military service, a requirement for all Mexican men, in order to qualify for a passport. He never made the effort. To top it off, the desert excursion of his took longer than expected because he was picked by "la migra" on the first try. In his mind, not having a passport, and getting picked up by ICE, was all my fault!

Fast Forward Another 1 ½ Years

We lived a pretty good life in Orange County, away from his family. But immigration laws became more strict, and due to his entanglement with homeland security a year and half earlier, the ex had been barred from the US for life. He was never going to be able to get legal papers, ever! Sadly, we headed back to Mexico.

The second time around, we rented a house across the street from a church. It was during that time, within just a few months of our arrival, that everything changed drastically. He had stopped working altogether, and I was the sole breadwinner, working two jobs, one on each side of the border. It was as if he had given up on everything – us, our marriage, his child, life in general.

In the house across the street from the church, he transformed the back room, behind the kitchen, into his man cave where he would spend almost all of his time. He kept that room under lock and key. While inside of the room, he sat in darkness. I set foot in that room only once, and that was more than enough. The negative energy emanating from the dark cave of his was so unbearable that I could barely handle going into the adjacent kitchen. I begged him to go to church with us, a church that was just a few feet away, yet he refused. I begged him to go to couples counseling, which he also denied me. I ran out of ideas on how to save the marriage, to save our little family, to save him. I didn't know what else to do until that wretched night, that is.

An ordinary night like any other, I had just put my son down to bed and I laid alone waiting to see how long it would take the ex to abandon his cave and join me. I eventually fell asleep. I was startled awake by the excruciating cries that sounded like a million wailing cats on the other side of the bedroom wall. When I tried to open my eyes, the porch light that had always shimmered in through the semi-sheer bedroom curtains blinded me. A light so bright that I had to use my forearm to shield my eyes. And the cats – their wailing pierced through my ears. I could hear nothing else. I could see nothing but the bright, blinding light. It was then, I realized I couldn't move. My body lay limp and practically lifeless next to a man who slept obliviously. There I was, in the dead of night – immovable, deaf, blind, and unable to breathe. I could feel my breath, shallow, while my body kept sinking heavier and heavier into the bed. I could feel my soul had begun to slowly drift away.

Thankfully, at that moment, my grandmother's magical words came to me, "I reject all evil." Because I couldn't scream or utter a single word, in my mind's eye I yelled these words with all my might as my fingertips gently swiped the palms of my hands. Slowly, I began to regain some movement, allowing me to swipe my way up my arms until I could reach my chest. With all of my strength, I cleared my chest and inhaled like a fish when thrown back into the deep blue sea. No sooner did I regain my breath, movement, and voice, when the ex sat up with eyes wide open. He turned to make direct eye contact and cussed me out. Within seconds, he had fallen back onto the mattress, his eyes closed, and began choking. I shook him, uncontrollably. He swatted me out of the way with his hand, cussed some more, and just like that, fell into a deep sleep and began to snore. Like magic, all returned to normal – no more wailing cats, no more blinding light, no more paralysis. The night had turned into a cold silence as I laid in disbelief.

Thereon after, every night, my son would wake up at some ungodly hour crying uncontrollably while pointing to the same wall. It still haunts me to think of all of the terrifying things my son may have witnessed during those surreal and haunting nights.

Within a matter of days, I sought out the help of a soothsayer to confirm what I already knew deep in my bones. An older woman, indeed, the one who had relentlessly tried to harm me was to blame. Without any guidance from the fortune-teller I sought out, everything began to make sense – the many obstacles I had continually encountered, all those years, by the ex's side had an answer. Despite the many challenges and inexplicable complications, I was told that I was well-protected and that this evil, older woman could not truly harm me as the evil spell she tried to hurt me with had evuientually landed on the ex, her own son. Many years had to pass in order for me to discover that the ex had been doing drugs the whole time we lived in the house across the street from the church. All of those years. I had no idea.

I rushed home to tell the ex that I was leaving with my son and that he was not joining us. I told him that his mother had won, that I wanted nothing to do with him or his family. Of course he dismissed the whole story. Who in their right mind would believe that their own mother had put a spell on them? The next day, I came home to find a suicide note from the ex detailing how he was going to take a drive up to la Rumurosa, and…experts say that when a suicide note includes a detailed plan, it is no longer a cry for help, but a serious threat. Well, I don't respond well to any kind of threats. If it had crossed his mind that I would feel so much of an inch sorry for him, he really had no idea who I was. The only thing he had stirred in me was deep-seated anger. How dare he threaten me! When I get angry, the fiery whirlwind inside of me makes mountains move. Within a few days, most of my belongings had either been sold or packed. I took my son, crossed the border, and never looked back.

Many, Many Years Later

The whole ordeal with the ex had been so traumatic for me that I couldn't bring myself to file for divorce. The thought of having to face the awful truths hurt too much. Filling out divorce documents would have forced me to admit that what I had lived was real – that my son and I really did run for our lives. In silence. No one knew what we had gone through. It was too frightening to recount. Plus, if I could barely believe what we had experienced, how in the world could I ever expect anyone else to believe the story? Years later, I finally filed for dissolution and disclosed the entire nightmare to my family. They had never imagined, or even had a clue, that my son and I endured such horrifying events. Sharing the story with my family was such a relief. I hadn't realized how heavy a burden I carried for all of those years. It wasn't until 2023 or 2024 that I actually wrote two poems about my lived experiences. Once again, another layer had been lifted. This chapter is the final release.

I am not crazy! I never was. This is my story. This is what I lived, and I wish it on no one else. All I can say to you is this: believe the signs, take head, do what only you know is best for you and your children (if there are children) learn to forgive yourself, and when you are ready, my hope is that you can learn to forgive those who hurt you. Not for their sake, but for your own healing. I grew up hearing that getting a divorce was a failure. No! Failure is not protecting our children. Failure is allowing our children to grow up in unhealthy and unsafe homes. My son's safety was and will always be far more important than anything else. I knew in my heart that we were better off alone.

The only regret I have is that I didn't have the know-how to understand the signs and warnings from my spirit guides. Since then, I have learned so much. I made a lot of mistakes along the way, but there is no doubt in my mind that I gave my son a much better life than the one he could have had if I stayed. As for me, there is an old adage in Spanish that I hold as my truth, "It is better to be alone than with bad company." Peace of mind, with or without company, is the greatest key to happiness, and that is my greatest wish for you.

'Tis not a Midnight Dreary

The screeching shrills did truly shatter
the hidden veil of human matter
on what appeared to be an ordinary night.

But this was not a midnight dreary
for I was fast asleep and weary
when the felines did cause such a terrible fright.

Heavily, my eyelids did shudder.
Not a single word could I utter.
Something very abnormal would prevent my sight.

Hesitantly, my eyes would open.
Though I tried, no word could be spoken
on such an ordinary, horrifying night.

~

My body could not move.
My breath began to lose
despite my willingness to fight.

My fingers touched my palms.
My mouth resounded psalms
as I began to pray with might.

~My grandmother's words, I remembered
whilst my living hours felt outnumbered.
"I reject all evil!" is what I did recite.

Slowly, my body regained movement.
My heavy breath felt great improvement
on such an ordinary, horrific night.

Surely, my senses, I recovered.
Gasping for air next to my lover
while he slept peacefully with delight.
No sooner did he begin to choke.
I shook and shook him 'til he awoke.
He sat up, looked at me, then cursed with all his might.

He laid back down for he was asleep.
I looked at him hard in disbelief.
He'd looked at me in the eye and cursed - oh, what a sight!

There laid my lover sleeping soundly
while I stayed up praying profoundly
trying to forget such a mortifying night.

To this day, that night still does haunt me.
Sometimes, I think that death still wants me
especially on this, an ordinary night.

She Made a Pact with the Devil

She never imagined how heavily protected I was.

During my pregnancy,
my blood pressure was through the roof,
yet I felt nothing.
I could have fallen into a coma,
but I didn't.
My liver could have ruptured,
but it didn't.

~

She never imagined how heavily protected my son was.

He was supposed to be a New Year's baby,
yet they had to induce labor
one month early.

He could have been incubated,
but he wasn't.
He could have had a slew of respiratory issues,
but he didn't.

~

She never imagined how unprotected her own son was.

My son and I were supposed to be her targets,
yet it was her son who suffered
the consequences of her own evildoing.

He could have fallen into a dark hole,
which he did.

He could have lost his wife and child,
which he did.
He could have consumed drugs to the point of extinction,
which he almost did.

~

And all because I loved her son.

(Both poems were first published in Conversaciones con los difuntos /
Conversations with the Dead, Editorial Desierto Mayor,
2024)

Diosa Xochiquetzalcóatl is currently serving as a board member for Círculo de poetas and Writers; works as a Poet-Teacher with California Poets in the Schools; and is an active member of Women Who Submit and the international women's poetry troupe, Tesoro. Diosa X has been published in a variety of anthologies and literary magazines in the U.S. and Mexico and is the author of seven poetry collections and one chapbook: A Church of My Own (2021), Hechizera: Sus Sultry Spells (Editorial Raíces, 2022), West of the Santa Ana and Other Sacred Places (Riot of Roses Publishing, 2023), Felices Fiestas (Read and Green Books, 2023), Conversations with the Dead / Conversaciones con los difuntos (Editorial Desierto Mayor, 2024), When the Leaves Come Tumbling Down: An A to Z Poetry Collection About Loss (Hawkeye Publishing, 2024), MeXicana: poemas y más poemas (Riot of Roses Publishing, 2025), and Sad Girl Soliloquies (2025). To learn more about her work, feel free to visit www.diosax.net

Chapter 7
A Fractured Fairytale

Once upon a time...

When young, many of us believe in fairy tales. "Once upon a time...and happily ever after." We all live the "once upon a time" but it is my observation that "happily ever after" seldom happens during some marriages and in my case only happened after divorce. I now live "happily ever after."

When I was asked to introduce our family to our congregation one Sunday, after fifteen years of marriage and four kids, I described my marriage as "We are happily married." "He is happy and I am married." I endured another ten years of being "married" because of the kids. I stayed in my marriage for the kids until the youngest left to attend university. However, I also got divorced for the kids. I moved from Belgium to the USA three months after I got married. I left my family, siblings, a great job, culture, friends, and a country that I loved. Upon arrival, just before Christmas 1991, my husband gave me an album by Kenny Loggins called "Leap of Faith" to memorialize the giant step of faith and trust I made on his behalf. While the title song "Leap of Faith" illustrated our Overture, little did I know that the second song on the album, "The Real Thing" would become my finale.

In "The Real Thing" Kenny Logins expresses the agonizing and painful reality of divorce. In the song he addresses his little girl and mentions her brothers. I have two girls and two boys and even now, after eight years of divorce, the heartfelt words of the song put me to tears. I feel the words were my dialogue to my kids. The lyrics represent one of the main reasons for my divorce being the right reason. The song shows the vulnerability, conflict, confusion, and loss of direction of a parent during divorce and the strength, courage, and honesty with self that is needed on the road ahead.

Once upon a time I had a spiritual experience and I felt my soul was pointing me to make the decision to marry. I knew it would be a challenging road because I foresaw an eventual move to the USA and leaving everything and everyone I knew behind. I didn't anticipate it to be so soon, but my husband's company transferred him back to the USA two weeks after our marriage. My immigration followed three months later.

My first year of marriage was an absolute hell. I missed my family terribly, I didn't know anybody, calling home was a dollar per minute and so it happened only one time each week and only lasted twenty minutes. I must have landed on fertile ground because I got pregnant within a week and within a few more weeks the threats started. Before my daughter was born I was told "If you leave me I will cut you up in a box and send you back home to Belgium" and after the kids were born I was mentally and emotionally kept hostage with "If you leave me you will never win." "If you go back to Belgium you will never see your kids again." While my husband rarely put hands on me physically, I came home to myself and realized that I was not that concerned about winning. Although, every time he hurt me, he lost a part of me and my heart. Of course the children were the biggest pull to stay and endure. As they started to grow up he would further pull my heart strings convincing me that if I went back home I would greatly disappoint my father, as I was the only one of the four siblings not divorced.

In the years to follow, I witnessed the red flags of a toxic relationship. I experienced constant criticism, disconnection from friends and family, control, different views and values, confusing conditional love, unpredictable mood swings, and anger issues. Gaslighting, blaming, disregarding boundaries, lack of respect, self righteousness, stubbornness, poor communication, and mental and emotional abuse were common. Each of these things, in their extreme, would qualify to make divorce the right answer.

I know that many women go through much more than a toxic relationship and feel judged for not making the move to step out of that pattern even when they are offered a way out. Why did I stay in the pattern? Why did I stay twenty-four more years and three more kids when the abuse qualified leaving after one year? There are many reasons why I stayed and waited before making the decision that divorce was the right answer. Some of these reasons might be seen as an explanation, some even an excuse to not rock the boat, and some were coping mechanisms I developed in order to keep going. Each is distinctive and personal in nature and represents my observation of life. There is no particular order although most of them are interconnected.

Loyalty, virtue, or vice

I must have been eleven years old when my mom, after four or five years of seeing another man, decided to move in with him. He had conquered her heart. We went to our home to pick up some of my mom's belongings, as well as those of my three siblings. The neighbor across the street alerted my dad that we were there and told him to come home to witness the move out. The first time my dad came home there was a physical fight which sent my mother's boyfriend to the emergency room as his hand needed stitches. Allegedly, he was my dad's good friend and obviously as a little girl I had picked up the cloud of betrayal and sadness in my home.

A few weeks later, I remember going home with my mom to pick up more of our belongings. This time my dad, fully aware, was sitting in a chair holding his defeated face in his hand which was supported by his elbow, resting on my mom's little sewing cabinet. I was sitting right across from papa, pleading, asking if I could stay with him.

He answered with a silent voice "You can't kinnekke" (a flemish term of endearment for little children) "Papa needs to go to work." At that moment, in what to most little girls might have seemed an insignificant event, my mom asked my dad to remove his arm from her sewing cabinet with the words "I am taking this too." The image of my dad, peacefully surrendering to my mom's request has replayed in my mind in slow motion for decades. Tears rolled over his face, something I only witnessed four times during his life. In this moment of pain, tears rolled over my cheeks and I proclaimed "Papa I want to stay with you, I will marry you" At that moment in time I made a vow to stay loyal, to not just my dad, but any future man, no matter what. My mom returned home after a few weeks and my parents stayed together despite their differences and unfulfilled relationship.

My parents' vow to stay loyal became a virtue in the sense of keeping commitments and promises. This translated into my vow to "Stay loyal to the Royal within." However, since I was young I could see the light or "royal" in other people, despite their choices, and I observed their wounds as blocks to the light within. My gift of finding the light in others ultimately took me on the path of mentor, soul coach, and energy practitioner in the healing arts, allowing me to help people to reconnect with their "royal" by clearing them of light stealing energy blocks. On the other hand, in my own loved ones and family, I abandoned myself, ran to their rescue, and stayed loyal to their "royal" instead of my own. When my marriage did not measure up to what I saw as its potential, my heart broke. Feeling misunderstood, I felt my relationship was a bouquet of flowers which was continually trampled ignorantly under foot rather than a relationship of beauty. Ultimately, losing myself in helping others brought more division than unity, not just in my marriage but also other relationships.

Along comes the spider

In my need to understand, my hope and a feeling of pride in fixing my husband, I looked for a better way to approach our situation. I went back to school, took classes, read books, consulted counselors, mentors, and wise friends. I learned to use new tools and consequently I decided to fly back in the spider's web, this time as a bigger fly and better prepared. Yet, the spider would meticulously suck away my energy and leave a dry corpse to drop to the ground. One day after a long training I decided to pick up my strength and courage and make another attempt, as a big bumble bee. Bees do not get stuck in spider webs very often because they are generally stronger and better fliers than a spider's usual feast. A bee would make a great meal for a spider but it's rarely worth the aggravation for most spiders. I thought I was "bumbled up" enough to conquer the web. I was wrong again, I felt attacked, sucked dry, and left empty. I realized my husband did not want to be fixed, and the result was that we grew further apart. We both felt broken and in need of healing.

A Martyr is a Victim with a Crown

I found it easy to fall into victimhood. I always had the desire to be a hero in someone else's life. I love hero stories and movies and favor those with heroine scripts. I have, however, observed that victims do not become heroes by staying in their victimhood. I also noticed that in certain cultures and religions people, particularly women, are revered and crowned for enduring suffering and pain. Personally, I developed a martyr complex. A pattern of self-sacrificing behavior and consistently putting the needs of others before my own. When I was young my mom told me that when I did a good deed for others God would put pearls on my crown. Not wanting to be a victim who throws my pearls to the swine, I was willing to suffer and self-sacri fice. I used my good deeds and service of others to collect my pearls. I started to measure my worthiness with how well I performed and my strength with how well I endured through the pain. I became a martyr, a victim with a crown. I felt I would surely be rewarded in heaven.

The Genesis Paradigm

Once upon a time...in the beginning...the origin...the coming into being of something...Genesis. The biblical and patriarchal, along with the fact that I was raised in a matriarchal family, are equally important. My mom and maternal grandma were both outspoken and overbearing. On the other hand, my parents adhered to religion with strong patriarchal teachings, explaining some of the conflict I witnessed during my childhood years as well as the conflict I experienced within an abusive marriage.

The Book of Genesis is the first book of the Hebrew Bible and the Christian Old Testament. Its Hebrew name is the same as the "first" word. It is interesting to observe that the "first" word in Hebrew describing the relationship between man and woman was translated in a patriarchal way. This yields to the strong gender superiority that I was conditioned to accept. After eating the apple, in Genesis 3:16, God assigns Eve her role and fate. "Unto the woman he said, I will greatly multiply thy sorrow and thy conception; in sorrow thou shalt bring forth children; and thy desire shall be to thy husband and he shall rule over thee." The Hebrew word for over was "Bet" with the letter H making it B'ezrat Hashem meaning "with the help of God" giving it an origin "and thy desire shall be to thy husband and he shall rule with thee."

I was not raised with, and never really believed in, strong gender roles such as male over female, one ruling over the other. Nevertheless most people, at some point, experience gender inequality. Once I experienced inequality in my marriage I recognized more division and less desire to connect. While not raised with this concept in my home, I still saw it lived in other ways in society. I also became familiar with the concept through religion. In my marriage, I saw how it thwarted the desire to connect and grow together.

Beliefs and Conditioning

Along with the foundational paradigm in the book of Genesis, from the moment of birth, people are programmed and conditioned into patterns, roles, behaviors, habits, routines, and cultural practices. The belief systems, views and opinions of our parents, care givers, family, teachers, authorities, and friends determine the way we look at life. Theis perception and the relationships people have with themselves, God, the Higher Power or the Divine, and the world are molded in early childhood. The first seven years of a child's life are marked with a period of rapid growth and development during which children's brains are primarily in a "theta brain wave state." Their highly receptive and suggestible brains are essentially "programming" their subconscious with beliefs and patterns that can significantly impact their future development and behavior as adults. I wonder if the conditioning I had as a child contributed to my situation.

Throughout life people are enticed, challenged, blinded and conditioned through conflicting messages about relationships, marriage, divorce and especially love. The media, television, social media, music, and other influencing platforms influence the mind. Lyrics like "I can't help falling in love, so take my hand and my whole life too"with its swiping and passionate melody might sound romantic, but living the lyrics, in my case, brought me to giving up my personal power. I became codependent which led to a broken heart. Eventually I started thinking, feeling, and acting like a victim with a crown. Equally so, my husband's beliefs, views and conditioning impacted the way he expressed his love. I believe he loved me. But in his fear of losing me and of me leaving him, he became overbearing, abusive, and controlling.

Going back to my early childhood years, I can most definitely see a pattern of deep rooted belief around relationships. These beliefs translated to high expectations of self, guilt and self-judgment. When I did not live up to those expectations, I started bullying myself into shame. I believed there was something wrong with me. Along with this lowered sense of self, came a fear to fail, and a fear of telling things to my parents. My parents lived five thousand miles away and I was afraid to disappoint them, especially my father who I always respected and sought approval from. Threats of abuse from my husband, his gaslighting, and my thinking it was my job to keep my husband happy were reasons that I stayed in an abusive marriage even when divorce was the right answer.

Wound Licker and Lion Tamer

My kids were the main reason I stayed married, and the reason for later seeking divorce. As the kids grew older and more independent, our parental views and opinions differed more and more. It is one thing to have different parenting styles. It is another when one of the parents, through their own conditioning and wounds, sees an authoritarian, controlling style of parenting and loving and the more relaxed, inspiring, and nurturing style of the other parent as enabling, irresponsible, and weak. This rift became a debatable field of who is right, who was wrong and what is considered good or bad within my marriage. It felt like I was living between two fires due to developing mental and emotional conflicts. I would correct the kids under the umbrella of teaching them what was right, and my husband utilized control by setting high expectations on performance without allowing choice.

In the beginning years, when the kids were young, it was harder to discern the disconnect and harm he was initiating. As the children became older and more independent, it became clear that I, as the mother, was not the only target for the emotional and mental abuse but the peacekeeper, licking the wounds of my cubs after yet another verbal attack. Once the cubs were calm, my next job was to tame the Lion, waiting in the bedroom for his caress. Needless to say, I no longer trusted my husband with our cubs and just as he intended, I would not leave him or home until the cubs were grown.

Even today, the kids have a tendency to feel as though they are not good enough. Some of them have a need for approval and they struggle because they tie worthiness to performance. Three of my four children asked me to leave their dad which ultimately gave me the courage to pursue the divorce. If my kids would have vetoed the break up, my loyalty, beliefs, conditioning, and co-dependency would most likely have kept me stuck. I am so glad they persisted.

My youngest son, the last to get married, divorced after six months. Some might observe the divorce as failure and quitting. Others might consider his decision an extension of "the sins of the parent to the child" and my bad example. No matter what others think, he learned from me not to compromise on real love and to have the courage to divorce before there were little humans involved and more hearts broken. After his divorce, five years after my divorce, he exclaimed "We are NOT a broken family because of the divorce. All of my kids agree that we were more broken as a family before the divorce. Divorce brought healing.

During the divorce

While most of the kids left home, my oldest daughter stayed under my wings due to a disability. During the five years prior to the divorce, I had been in a battle over our house due to the mortgage security fraud that began in 2007. To make matters worse, my husband lost his job four times, causing us to lose all of our savings. Additionally, our 401K tanked. We had been foreclosed on three times and in the last of two short sales, 1 week after my youngest left for university, we lost the beautiful house we had built ten years prior. The positive side of the loss was that we had less in common and one less thing to fight over. The hard part was that my husband moved in with family in town and I was left without shelter with all of my family being overseas. Luckily a sweet lady from my church rented me a beautiful home for a low price, one that I could afford. My other daughter and my youngest son moved back home for six months after which my son left on a service mission for our church, my daughter got married, and I had to move out again as our house was sold. This time, I moved my belongings into storage and started working in a holistic hospital in Mexico where I worked three months on and three months off. A busy time of travel between Mexico and the USA, my disabled daughter and I stayed with my married daughter, during my off-months, for nearly a year-and-a-half. After my job at the holistic hospital was complete, we stayed with a dear friend in Idaho as preparation for finding and moving into a new home.

The Aftermath

The first year after the divorce my x-husband, in scorn, would continue to throw darts. He met another woman and married her within the first year. He didn't spare me any pain for another six years.

All of these inflictions took me to what I call my "suicide closet" where I plead with God to return me home to Him.

I had sent the Divine my resume, listing all of my attributes, experiences, and good deeds as a friend, mother, wife, daughter, and employee, hoping to qualify for a job on the other side of the veil. I was alone and mightily cried to heaven. In a moment of despair and total surrender I felt a warm presence and heard a voice whispering in my mind "Linda you have to reverse your thinking" "You are not a human that is here to have a spiritual experience" "You are a soul, a spirit, having a human experience"

From that pivotal moment of bearing my soul to God in my closet, came a complete change in perception, thoughts in my mind, and a change of feelings in my heart. It was an experience that would forever change my life and those of uncountable patients, clients, and friends. Out of my painful experiences I developed "The Simple Principle," a map of the soul that helps people reconnect with their true identity, helps them see how painful experiences are degrees in life preparing us for our own purpose and dreams. The map acknowledges that the people and things that hurt us are teachers in the school of life. Experiences that are here to bring us messages to show us where we need to heal and find love. Healing comes when we meet our wounded places with compassion. When we do, our wounds become our superpowers, we become the alchemist in our own lab, the healer in our own body, the oracle in our own temple and the Hero on our own stage.

Sleeping Beauty becomes the Hero

Once upon a time... there was a princess who needed a hero
She traveled the seas and climbed mountains
She finally found the one
Brought to her by fire
She could see his light

They started a life of loving and learning
Conquering their challenges and finding solutions for their
problems
They multiplied in number but also in differences
Soon the mountain to high to climb alone

First the princess tried to calm the storms
A peacekeeper licking wounds and taming the lion
Carrying the weight on her shoulders
Hidden under an invisible burkha of shame and fear
She searched for the Light

Just like a caterpillar and a water nymph
She looked for the Light lateral within her view
Because of budget cuts
The Light at the end of the tunnel was turned off
She now looked UP
And followed the Light of the Sun

In the day she would find comfort, warmth and shelter
Basking in the Sun
At night in the darkness she cried
Where is Thy pavilion, Thy hiding place and shelter in the
storm

He heard her whisper underneath her breath
And answered
Slow down and Hear me

Be Still Be still and know the I AM is God

From her prayer closet, hidden beneath her broken heart
She heard her Hero and Master
Teaching her to further explore the Light and mastery within

She continued climbing every mountain and sailing different seas
This time to find the Light stolen and given
Tracing her back to the Light and hero within

The princess inspired by Sleeping Beauty
Waited patiently for a prince in golden armor
Giving her the redeeming kiss
To be awoken by a strange creature, a dragon
She recognized through his corresponding breath

"This is it" She exclaimed
I'm no longer waiting
I'll find the hero inside of me
I'll search and slay my dragons
Cut the thorns to find my weathering rose
Waiting for my redeeming love"

She came home to herself
Crowned with a Golden Heart
For the courage on the killing fields

She continues her travels
Her adventures of the heart
With her soul leading
Her compass is pointing her in a new direction
When the winds start blowing hurricane rejection
She trims the sails and goes in flow

In the flow
The colors of the wind have taught her
Resistance is the other half of momentum
Rejection means Redirection

Like the water nymph going through the long larval stage
Taking form as a beautiful dragonfly
Like the caterpillar going through the painful process of liquifying
She became a butterfly ready to take flight

The princess tried to calm the storms
She learned to calm the princess in the storm

She needed a hero..
So she became one

Healing through breaking

As a soul having a human experience in a human body, painful experiences are no longer stumbling blocks, but stepping stones to dreams and purpose. In The Purpose Driven Life, Rick Warren uses the SHAPE test, an acronym for Spiritual Gifts, Heart, Abilities, Personality, and Experience, he addresses the painful experiences as those God uses to prepare for our "ministry" because God never wastes pain. We are not broken down, but broken open through our painful experiences. We find strength in the struggle. We are face to face with our troubles when we are broken.

During trying times I think of the lyrics of the song "Broken" by Lindsey Haun from the movie "Broken Bridges." The lyrics support the beauty of finding the broken pieces of self and rebuilding a beautiful new you.

Happily Ever After...

Yes, tears were shed, hearts were broken, dreams were shattered, doubts were paramount, loss (even financial) was a reality, but a bigger deficit would have been to continue in a relationship without love, without joy, living with conditional and conditioned love.

Writing my story and about my experience with divorce has not been an easy task. I have had to let go of my narrative and rewrite my script, my story. I no longer hold any grudges and have felt true forgiveness in my heart. I look back with fondness to the good times I had. I have become the woman I am not despite my pains, but because of them. In the school of life, he was definitely my master teacher. While he may have caused heart injuries and heart breaks, he triggered and opened some childhood wounds showing me where I needed healing and more love. At first, I looked for healing in another man, only to be left with a deeper heart cavity, until I took my power back. I did my own inner healing and wound binding. I dared to see the balance between my challenges and losses. I now live my Happily Ever After.

Closing and Opening Night

On the closing night of my own play, just before the curtain falls, the players showed up on stage one more time. One by one they each get a standing ovation for their excellent performance in the play of life. I smile, go home, and enter my "suicide closet" to thank the Divine for the experiences of life, the players that brought me messages of what had to die for me to receive more love.

As the economy of the theater requires, there will be a new opening soon, presenting a play with a new story, a new narrative, a new cast, and a new set. When the curtain rises again on the opening night of my new play, I will present new characters. My sisters, kids and their spouses and partners, will be cast without audition. Others, including the main male character will be carefully selected and bring me new messages. As I look into the mirror the "new" will help me grow, expand, and become the hero on my own stage.

Credits

Master teacher 1:   ex-husband
After seven years of separation we are now on good terms, we have Christmases together with all the kids and have a lot of fun. His wife made his dreams come true, assisting him in a long anticipated five month ride on his bike across the USA from west coast to east coast.
His kids are on better terms with him, and we both are living our own happily ever after.

Master teachers 2:   my parents,
They woke me up to my true self and helped me free myself from self-judgment and approval
They both are on the other side of the veil. I feel them, I thank them and I connect with them on a regular basis. The world measures parenthood by how well the kids turn out. I measure parenthood by how well I turn out. My kids are and will continue to be master teachers that is why they will be in the sequel, my next masterpiece.

Oldest daughter: my special Angel
She teaches me so much about expectations, true love, and forgiveness. She continues to amaze me with her emotional intelligence and wisdom. She teaches Zumba, has a boy

friend with Down Syndrome and both of them bring us all joy and laughter.

Second daughter: a little "me" with a lot more spunk
From a very young age she mothered not only her older sister but her younger brothers. From our family dynamic she developed perfectionism and a tendency of never feeling good enough. She is very smart and intelligent and she has a heart of gold for people less fortunate than her and she is a lover and rescuer of animals. I learned from her to stand up for myself and free myself from martyrdom, wound licking and lion taming.

Oldest son: my warrior and protector
He is the one that had a very hard time with the divorce. He helped me from very young to see his father in a new light. He defended him and loved him even when his father was so hard on him.
He is learning to step in his own power and become his own authority.
If I could only take one thing in an emergency, it would be him. I know I would be safe, taken care of, protected, and sheltered.

Youngest son: my Innovator
When he was born I immediately felt the grandeur of his spirit. He is a leader, an innovator to pave the way for something new. He was often the target of criticism from his father. He has the most beautiful heart towards women. After the conflict in the family and his short marriage he armored his heart. He teaches me determination and to never give up. He inspires me to continue to believe in myself.

Next Chapter

We all suffer separation and divorce of some kind. Voluntary or involuntary, we go through losses, heartbreaks, and pain. Years ago I read a report that stated that people are more likely to divorce their spouse than their boss. I hope that my words will give you, the reader, the courage to take your power back and be the hero in your own story and the alchemist in your own lab.

Linda Verheyen, a native of Belgium with a global perspective shaped by years living in England and France, now calls the Western US home. Fluent in Dutch, French, and English, Linda's life's purpose is dedicated to helping individuals unlock their inner light. Through her unique approach of "energetic tune-ups and alignments," she guides clients towards lives filled with joy, peace, enlightenment, and abundance. Utilizing energy psychology and healing, Linda taps into the subconscious mind, believing that the innate intelligence within each person far surpasses any external learning, empowering them to realize their highest potential.

Chapter 7
Third Time is the Charm!

Like any teenager, I had a few boyfriends when I was back home. I lived with my family in Hato Rey, San Juan, Puerto Rico. Puerto Rico is part of the United States, a tiny island in an archipelago located in the Caribbean Sea. I got tired of living there, possibly due to Attention-deficit/ hyperactivity disorder (ADHD), so I enlisted in the US Army. Being in the Army was a culture shock. The weather and language were different and racism was an actual thing! On my home island we are a mixed race of white, black, and brown. Skin color is not much of an issue with the exception of some high school bullies who used to call me "Casper" and not because I reminded them of the cute "friendly ghost."

At any rate, after basic training, I was sent to a new post for specialized training. I was training as an orthopedic specialist. #1's training there (I will refer to my exes as #1, #2, and #3 to protect their privacy) was to become a combat medic. When it came to men, I was always attracted to action movies and liked light eyes. My father had light green eyes, and most of the boys back at home had them brown. One day, in military formation #2's formation was facing mine. I froze when I saw a muscular, green-eyed, handsome young man with an Airborne Ranger, striking maroon, beret! My Army experience led to my first time leaving Puerto Rico for more than a family trip. My references to the mainland United States were mostly from movies. #1 being an Airborne and a Ranger was real life Rambo sh*#! My eyes were glued to his face and my heart started beating quickly! I was happy, yet embarrassed! He looked so proud. Just like the GI Joe my brother would play with at home! Fortunately, #1 started looking and smiling at me when the platoon leader was not watching.

We started seeing each other whenever we could. Dating is kind of tricky when living in military barracks. We were separated by gender. I'm unsure how they do it now, but when I was there barracks were strictly "female" and "male" as the Army wanted to avoid any potential sexual contact. Remember, most of us went into the Army right after High School or mid-college like me. The Army's priority was to train us to be specialists in the medical field in one of two specialties. #1 and I could only see each other during a few, specific, times. Gladly, we would all eat in the same chow hall and during after duty hours we could shine our boots in a common area, go to the military shoppette, etc. Since I was halfway through a bachelor's degree, my entry rank among the enlisted was grade three, Private First Class (E-3).#1 was a Private (E-1). I had a little bit more freedom than him. That is, instructors were not as rigid or focused on me.

#1 was very charming, clean, and respectful to me. We would hang out and I loved to sing Paula Abdul's "Forever Your Girl." It felt so real! I had finally found my prince charming! After some time, we went to City Hall and got married. I was a certified nursing assistant (CNA) in a Nursing Home in Tacoma, Washington, and an Air Medic in the Washington Air National Guard. Time went by and I got pregnant. We were so excited! However, I had to drop the last class for my associate's degree. Nevertheless, we went to my island for a family vacation. Everything was okay until we came back home.

Somehow, #1 started having problems in the Army. I had finished my Army contract and was puzzled when he would not explain what was happening with his career. I think that he did not want to worry me as I was pregnant. All I know is that he started acting erratic. He was still polite with me but very unpredictable. I was tired from working the graveyard shift, 11pm to 7am, and being in the guard while pregnant.

One day, during breakfast, he announced that he had been kicked out of the Army! All I could think was

"Oh my God, now what?" We started looking for options. I asked my boss to hire #2 as he had a medical background. My boss hired him and trained him just as they did with me. Staff typically handled nine seniors during shifts. Since #1 was very fit, he was asked to work during the day.

It was a shock when somehow he was fired again. One night, during my first trimester, I went to the bathroom. All of a sudden I started bleeding and became dizzy. I managed to pull the emergency cord in the bathroom. All I remember is waking up in the hospital. Doctors had performed a "dilation and curettage (D&C)" to remove the dead fetus from my body. It was a horrible day for me – for us.

Despite my jobs we were forced to file for debt consolidation followed by bankruptcy! I was used to seeing my parents with a joint account, so I had trusted #1. Now, I had to apply for government coupons in order to eat! Of course I appreciated the coupons and I do not look down on people who must use them. It is just that I had been raised in an upper middle class family. My father was a physician and my mother was a dietitian. I felt that I had let them down and knew that they would now worry and suffer for me.

One day I came home from work to read an eviction notice on the front door of our little apartment. When I got inside, Puffy, the puppy I had brought with me from Puerto Rico, was barking a lot. A group of four or five men started knocking on my door. #1 was not home and I was scared! I thought the men had come to steal from us and rape me. Fortunately, my dog stopped barking when I grabbed a trophy I had won in a martial arts competition on my island. We stayed quiet and they left, commenting that I was not there.

The cherry on top, the sour one, was the day when I returned from work and #1 and the neighbor were sitting at the top of our neighbor's roof. Both men were smoking crack! To top it all off, the #%!()*$ dared to sell Puffy and most of the furniture!

I went to the nearest recruiting office and re-enlisted in the Army, full-time. When I reported to the barracks I got a call from #1's parents, whom I had never met, begging me to take him back. I felt for them, but I had gone through the worst ten months of my life! I went to the judge advocate, an Army lawyer, to get divorced. They told me that because our relationship was less than a year-long and we were no longer living together or having contact the marriage would be annulled. #1 was served with annulment papers from the court and I have yet to return his calls to this day. I finally made the logical connection that #1's parents were ministers preaching from state to state due to their personal and professional goals and that he had grown up in multiple orphanages. I have no problem with their ministry; I am studying to become a reverend. However, I believe that #1 grew up in sadness knowing that he had a pair of healthy parents who chose their callings over him.

In the end, I ghosted #1 and it gave me a lot of time to think over the many losses in my life. For example, my "Disney World dream" was already shut down as I thought being married was a one-time thing! Losing my baby, whether it was a whole being yet, or not, was traumatic. I had a copy of an ultrasound showing a heartbeat. Waking up in a hospital feeling a scraped bleeding uterus was horrible. I had not planned for that! Yet somehow I felt guilty, like I should have taken better care of my belly.

Yes, I blame having to care for nine elderly patients, in a nursing home, for the loss. Maybe when I was lifting residents to bathe them, I had caused the miscarriage. Feeling responsible for the miscarriage made it all worse. I was willing to help the residents and their families, but I should have taken better care of myself or quit!

I was also grieving my other baby, Puffy. She was the daughter of our family poodle and my sister's Maltese. Today, many decades later, even with my new poodle a few feet from me, my eyes get watery. I feel sad that Puffy trusted me and I could not protect her from being taken away! Like any mom, I was supposed to keep her safe and loved! I prayed that she did not end up with some drug addict living on the streets who might continue selling her forward. I hope she instead found a good mother and child, in a loving and safe home. That's what I asked the angels to find for Puffy. Now that I am a developing medium, I have also asked Puffy directly for forgiveness.

The annulment hurt because #1 was someone I had trusted for so long, less than a year, but more than three months! In addition to Puffy, I lost many things I brought from Puerto Rico, like photos and clothes. I would never have those things again, especially my family photos. I could only hope there were copies back at home. All of these experiences made me stronger and at the same time less trusting. I was sad and hurt, so I focused all of my energy and time on my new full-time military job. In the military we often had to go to the field for experiences that lasted about a month which kept me very busy. At the end of each day I was ready to go to my military cot and sleep. I know now that I should have built myself up more after #1, because I soon met #2 while living in the Army barracks. #2 wanted to meet me. I was not that interested but felt pressured and I felt sorry for him. Everything was great in the beginning. However, I could see how other women would look at him and vice versa. #2 and I ended up getting married by a non-denominational minister in someone's backyard.

On our honeymoon night, after roses and the typical romantic time, #2 told me he was going to go out with his friends. Clear dominance. I felt demoralized but I did not want to hurt our relationship by asking him to stay. From then on I realized what a neurotic animal he was. One day we had a couple coming over and I went to the bedroom to change clothes. The sweater #2 bought for me fell on the floor. Oh my God! He yelled at me like I had killed someone. How embarrassing! Again, I was not raised like that. Yes, Puerto Ricans tend to talk loud and move their hands. Many people think (as you will see with #3 ahead) that we are arguing when we are not. However, this guy was crazily screaming at me! For a stupid sweater touching the ground! I realized quickly that his hang-up with clothes was the fact that he was brought up in poverty. It was imperative for him to have clean, flashy brand name shirts, shoes, and cars because it was an outward projection of his financial success. In my home the only expectation of me was to wear uniforms to private schools and military academies and a dress for church. Unfortunately, I was continually belittled within the relationship. #2 would say things like "You can't cook, so you are never gonna find anyone other than me." "You are clumsy," and eventually these words began to break my spirit.

On Christmas night we went to eat with another couple. I remember that I had hot dogs with cheese and we went to get ice cream. After having ice cream we were alone in "his truck" as he would regularly remind me. He started criticizing me, again, about who knows what. Maybe I was breathing "wrong" that day. I started throwing up. I am unsure if becoming ill was the combination of spicy, hot, and sweet food, or just a mechanism of defense to push everything away, including him. I ended up in the Emergency Room. I remember a lovely man dressed like Santa Claus giving me hot cocoa in a Santa cup. I kept that cup.
I don't know why but becoming ill continued to happen. I noticed that every time he started belittling me I would start throwing up. I thank God that I never got pregnant! I would not want to raise a child with someone with his neurotic genes.

One night #2 wanted to have sex and he was jumping on me as I fought him off. I am 5"1' and when I married him I weighed 115 pounds. That weight, due to my situation, dropped down to 99 pounds. #2 was 6'2" and 210 pounds. I was no match for him as he grabbed me by the neck and banged my body against the wall. It felt like he was choking me to death. I kept kicking him and praying. He finally let go and took off in his stupid truck, blasting music. I took the opportunity to grab a little suitcase and my new puppy, "Rambo." I ran to my neighbor's house and begged her not to share my whereabouts.

I never wanted to bother my parents after I left home. I wanted them to be proud of me and my progressive individuality. They still had my brother home, and I would rather they take care of him instead of worry about me. However, I was so desperate that I called my dad crying. I told him that I only had three hundred dollars in my purse. He told me, calmly and lovingly, not to worry about anything and to go straight to the airport. He would take care of everything. I did so.

I must confess, I cried all of the way home. I felt like such a failure. I still remember looking through the window, hoping #2 would see me, magically apologize, and make everything better. Rambo was tiny, so he was allowed to be in my lap for which I was thankful.

When I arrived in Puerto Rico I was emaciated and my family was horrified. Let's say it took me a few times before I could watch the whole movie Sleeping with the Enemy. I was Laura Burney! Whenever I saw a man who looked like #2 I would freeze and panic. He kept calling me and trying to manipulate me into "going home with him." That place was no longer home. It was not a safe place. However, due to his calls, I started planning for him to visit us. My father, in his wisdom, did not want #2 around. A few times, I felt like giving in to #2 and going back.

I moved in with my sister and shortly after someone jumped the fence and stole Rambo. Not again! I had already had one dog taken from me and it had been devastating. I could not handle losing another one of my furry babies! Rambo was gone and just as I did with Puffy, I prayed that Rambo ended up with another loving family.I prayed for their sake and mine, so I would stop feeling powerless and obsessing over my loss.

In the midst of my loss I was walking with my dad back to his office. He said calmly and lovingly, "Ok, go back to him, but promise you will finish your bachelor's degree." When he said that I felt like the world had stopped. As much as he loved me, and had suffered for me, he felt I had the tools to be strong on my own if needed. I remember immediately telling him that I was not going back. I felt empowered and I enrolled back in college. My dad paid my tuition for nearly two years. Since I like being proud of caring for myself I took over the bank payments.

As with #1, I only lived with #2 for ten months. Was it coincidence, serendipity, or meant to be? I was fortunate as one of my sisters was an excellent lawyer. She was ethical and had watched me struggle and suffer due to mistreatment during the marriage. She took my case and arranged a hearing. My sister asked for a divorce based on cruelty. #2 was served divorce papers and despite his size and rage, he didn't have the balls to come to the island and confront my sister, my father, and me! I did not return his calls or love letters. I ghosted him.

Both the annulment and the divorce were the correct answers in my life. I was young and impressionable. I had been protected from racism and cultural disparity during my youth in Puerto Rico. I was vulnerable and both #1 and #2 had abused my trust, my body, and my spirit. I survived severe loss, belittling, gaslighting, physical, emotional, and mental abuse. Divorce was the right answer for me. Everything has a beginning and an end and in my case the end of these relationships led to new beginnings in my life.

We are born alone, and we will die alone. Think about it, marriage is a contract. No vow says that partners must become clones of one another. Based on my experiences I would like to share some advice. After a career in psychology, I now recommend going to marital counseling to help solve problems in a relationship. If you happen to marry young like I did, I recommend avoiding pregnancy right away to allow the new relationship to mature. If a couple is already pregnant or has a child, or children, family counseling is still an option. In an abusive relationship where counseling doesn't work, get out of the relationship. Your child, or children, will thank you even if the family is split as they will be free of pain and mistreatment. Keep reaching out to family members who care for you. Avoid isolation. People who know you best will want to help you find happiness again. I have learned a lot about empowerment. Empowering others is my main goal as a coach and counselor. Eleanor Roosevelt said, "No one can make you feel inferior without your consent." When I was finding my own empowerment, I would sing songs like "Respect" by Aretha Franklin, "Believe" by Cher, "Stronger" by Kelly Clarkson, and "Roar" by Katty Perry.

I learned to exercise empathy and self-love. For example, after the annulment I concluded that #1 had grown up in sadness. His parents had chosen a life without him. It may have felt normal for him to leave places, people, and things. #2 was raised in a family where they did not have much at home, consequently, his drive to wear flashy clothes and drive loud cars would prove his success in life. I forgave both men and I hope they have forgiven me for any wrongdoing. I was mad for a while. However, I ended up looking for what I wished for everyone else in my life. I wished for them to live the best life they could without hurting anyone along the way. Life is too short to hold grudges. Be healthy and happy. Reach out for help if needed.

Now for the rest of the story! The third time's a charm! After ten years, I married an incredible man! My husband is incredibly loving and respectful and he protects our daughter, our dog, and me! He supported my military career despite having to move and quit many jobs. Furthermore, when I was traveling, or deployed in Iraq and Korea, he was both mom and dad to our daughter. He stood by my side throughout my fight with breast cancer and painful treatments. Despite his own cancer journey, he is still with me as I battle Stage 4, terminal cancer. The statistics suggest I only have two to five years of life left. However, the years with my husband and family have been the best twenty five years of my life! I pray to live way longer than statistics suggest and be here for my family. If I can't, I will care for them in the afterlife!

I wish the best to you and yours! You can do it!

Melba del Carmen Victoria Stetz Flores, Ph.D., LTC (Ret.), CYT, BCN, BCB has three degrees in Psychology and many board certifications. She was born in Puerto Rico and worked in the three Americas as part of the United States ARMY.

She is a published author (https://scholar.google.com/citations? USAer=fOhhu-oAAAAJ) and a motivational speaker/coach. Her latest publication (in both English and Spanish) is "Healing Talks- A Dying Patient's Story (https://www.amazon.com/author/melbastetz).

Email: drmelbastetz@gmail.com
Website: https://drmelbastetz.com
LinkedIn: https://www.linkedin.com/in/dr-melba-stetz/

Chapter 8
How To Lose Five Wives

Repetitive Downfall

1978-1981 (ages 18-21)

The first one thought monogamy was monotony
Convinced her to get married and have the baby
After an argument I picked up a date at Music Plus
Confessed to my already cheating confessing wife
She moved on with the next in her series of lovers
A blind guy she seduced who lived by the beach
She took the car but not our son.

1982-1990 (ages 22-30)

The second indulged my new-found voyeurism
Posed starkers in hotel room windows
Ran jaybird around a midnight parking lot
We did it once by a freeway on ramp
I played footsie with her best friend at school
Kissed our next-door neighbor
Had an affair with a coed
She lost her job and left her husband on the same day

1991-2010 (ages 31-50)

Third was an unhappy drunk because of teenage unwanted
child guilt
She played footsie with her niece's husband
She hugged him at her mother's funeral
She loved exposing cleavage to potential male skin care
clients
She had an emotional breakthrough with an older man
Internet porn became my companion
Also neglected, a married woman entered my life
She just so happened to be a massage therapist
I left my wife to be closer to her

2011-2016 (ages 51-56)

By dating site luck, I'm with an-
other massager
Who brags about earning big tips
Two months into our marriage I
uncovered
Who her weekend roommate
was, her not quite ex
I let her stay because I loved her
We decide to buy a house togeth-
er
She changed her mind and went
to live with
A far older richer man with
MASH residuals

2017-2020 (ages 57-60)

My massage friend introduces me to a shy woman
Who promises we will have a sex life
Only when we get married
After the ceremony she goes home
I am alone on my wedding night
A WeChat message from me declares
You don't come here I file for divorce
She came but lived in a separate bedroom
I never saw her naked let alone have sex
She moved back to her rented room

Aftermath

First wife
She filed for divorce
I started dating a coworker

Second Wife
She filed for divorce
I met a woman at a payphone

Third Wife
We actually never married
So no paperwork here

Fourth Wife
We went to the courthouse together
To file the fastest divorce you ever saw

Fifth Wife
Two days after she left
A man came to my door and served me

Rebuild

First Wife
I exercised to The Who's "You Better You Bet"
Flattered a coworker had her eyes on me

Second Wife
I went looking for a new partner
Found someone more troubled than me

Third Wife
I realized you can't marry a married woman
Signed up for a free dating website

Fourth Wife
More online dating then
My married friend introduced me

Fifth Wife
After several failed relationships
Met a woman who was as interested in me as I was in her

Forward Motion

Five Wives
When you have an irreconcilable difference
That is never going to change or be forgotten
Go forward, don't go back
Moving on is the only way to be happy again

If it's a simple agreed-upon divorce
Print out your own papers
No need for a lawyer
Then get out there and meet people (if you feel like it)

Don Kingfisher Campbell, MFA in Creative Writing from Antioch University Los Angeles, taught Writers Seminar at Occidental College Upward Bound for 36 years, been a coach and judge for Poetry Out Loud, a performing poet/teacher for Red Hen Press Youth Writing Workshops, L.A. Coordinator and Board Member of California Poets In The Schools, poetry editor of the Angel City Review, publisher of Four Feathers Press, and host of the Saturday Afternoon Poetry reading series in Pasadena, California. For awards, features, and publication credits, please go to: http://dkc1031.blogspot.com

Chapter 9
I Married a War Refugee

I married a war refugee. Born of exile, of fight or flight, of run-before-they-catch-us. Made of fugitive grief taller than the Himalayas, adrenalin explosions, machete-in-hand-fears, prickly paranoias. He came from a place that smells of jack fruit, green coconut water, and monsoon petrichor. Also, a town textured by midnight massacres, blood-stained rice fields, hyenas gnawing on corpses: the messy ripples of India's partition.

At nineteen, I didn't see his realities. Instead, I saw big brown eyes full of dreams adorning the face of the man I loved. Never mind that we met in a yoga ashram where he had been a monk for twelve years, or that neither of us had a college diploma or a penny to our names, or that my Dad, at first, strongly objected to our union. In Vijay, my romantic heart saw the man I longed to wed, the father of my future children, my destiny, my everything.

Vijay grew up in the verdant hills just south of Bangladesh. His family settled there after sneaking across the Meghna River by moonlight, cobras underfoot, sights set east of Dhaka, away from the violence that had ravaged their village. I grew up in the land of the Tenochca people, where live volcanoes rimmed our urban valley and roads turned into rivers when it rained. Vijay and I both came from conch-shell-blowing, incense-burning, fire-igniting rain summoners on opposite sides of the planet. Whether it was Tlaloc or Indra creating the downpours, we bonded over a mutual love for monsoons. On rainy nights Vijay and I would stay up late holding hands in our matrimonial bed, unraveling stories to the sound of raindrops. Plunging into nostalgia and pretty pictures, we imagined our future together. I should have known then that the sparse rain of the Southern California desert we called home would not sustain us for long.

Sometimes, marriages dwindle over time like beach cliffs eroding with the constant ebb and flow of tides. Other times, there may be a tsunami that wipes everything away at once. Our marriage suffered several tidal waves in quick succession. Death, followed by robberies, followed by more death. Vijay would wake yelling from grief triggers and nightmares about dodging dacoits, bullets, bombs, the swing of a sharp sword. How does one survive witnessing the slicing-in-half of a child? Or a row of corpses resting on the dirt road you took to school? It wasn't until ten years into our marriage, as we grieved our unborn daughter, that I knew I had married a child of war. Even after having successfully escaped a place of genocide, genocide still lived in him, in my Vijay, ever intent on decimating us.

War crimes cannot be unseen. One of Vijay's stories in particular, stands out: the slaughter of the tea farmer's family. Vijay watched his mother's silhouette against the moonlight – a crouched figure in the open doorway, tightly clutching a machete in her hands the night after the killings. Every time the jasmine-scented wind kicked up the violet cloth that hung in place of a door, Vijay jumped, fearing for his life. Would his family be next?

Little Usha survived only because she had been tiny enough to slip under one of the short bamboo cots they slept on. That's where the police officers found her the next morning: trembling in a puddle of her parent's blood. Walking to school, Vijay spotted Usha, just about his age, sitting alone on a wooden bench outside the police station—blood splatter on her dress, a symbol of everything he wanted to flee. The glossy look in Usha's dark eyes haunted Vijay into adulthood. That same night, Vijay made a makeshift piggy bank by cutting a little slit into the top of one of the bamboo rods supporting his home's roof. Every time Vijay came across a paisa or, better yet, a rupee, he slipped it into the slot. Whenever Vijay grew anxious, he put his ear to the bamboo pole and knocked on it. The less hollow it sounded, the closer he felt to safety. At fourteen, Vijay had saved enough coins to buy his first pair of shoes and a train ticket to Calcutta.

I met Vijay thirteen years later. He was a head-shaven, saffron-robed monk with a thick Indian accent and fabulous storytelling skills. I was an easily enamored teenager attending his yoga philosophy classes. With hands that moved like birds and Sanskrit song peppering his narratives, Vijay transported his audiences to the banks of sacred rivers in Bengal, the snowed-in hermitages of Himalayan sages, and lotus flowers large enough to sit in. I wanted to listen to him forever! Four months later, Vijay and I snuck off to apply for our marriage license. For the first few years of our marriage Vijay, who was ten years older than I, made me feel like Princess Jasmine on a flying carpet-ride, being introduced to "A Whole New World." Little did I know that our magical ride had an expiration date.

A friend once told me that it's not so much the experiences we have that shape us, but the stories that we tell ourselves about them. Unbeknown to me, Vijay had a story in him that ended up being much stronger than our marriage: his cobra bite story! Every time he told the story of the bite, his eyes widened like two dark moons. Once, as a young boy, Vijay woke up to find himself lying on the dirt courtyard outside his home, surrounded by wailing relatives and townsfolk. They were all terrified that Yamaraja, death personified, hovered above to collect Vijay's soul. The mystical healer wasted no time in tying a rope to Vijay's big toe and pulling on it with fierce jolts. Vijay would say, "I was sure my leg was going to come off!" Hours later, a miracle happened: The cobra returned and withdrew the venom from Vijay's leg with a second bite! The crowd cheered, the child roused, and from his mother's grateful arms little Vijay overheard the snake charmer say "One who survives the bite of a cobra, is destined to become either an opulent king or a renounced sadhu!" But, giving a child two extremely opposite futures is bound to confuse. I watched Vijay oscillate between his two true norths for years.

When I fell in love with the sadhu, I missed the small print that said I was required to become a queen, a Laxmi Devi, a goddess of fortune. As a little girl I didn't see myself as a princess living in a castle. My preferred ceiling was sky, my Persian carpet soft earth. I was happiest sitting between lava rocks in Mami's garden, telling stories to lizards, making mud cakes under pink bougainvillea vines. My dreams were of becoming a danzante with feathers in my hair, feet synced with drums. Or a painter like Frida Kahlo, whose Caza Azul was just around the corner from our own casa. Later, when I was eleven, I dreamed of writing flower songs like Nezahualcoyotl, whose poems we read aloud in school. I'd stay up with the moon and write into the night until my mother would catch me and tell me to get in bed, turn off my light, and remind me that it was a school night.

Vijay's childhood dreams, however, weren't as whimsical. He was, after all, the boy who had survived a cobra's bite. And none of the villagers ever let him forget it. So, when Vijay lay in bed at night under a bamboo thatched roof, he pictured himself as a gold-chain-wearing Bollywood star living in a big mansion. Modern royalty, as it were. Other nights he saw himself as a barefoot guru in tangerine robes reciting mantras under a tree. This conflict of interests followed Vijay into adulthood. Should he acquire riches or take poverty vows? When one path frustrated him, he'd abort and zoom down the other.

I entered Vijay's life when he was at one such impasse. He gave up his monkhood to marry me, a Mexican girl. Then, the night after our marriage, Vijay called me from a payphone sobbing with regret. If that wasn't a foreshadowing of things to come, I don't know what is. Looking for the silver lining, he'd later say, while eating my tortillas and beans, that our cultures were very similar. But our values weren't. When making money in America, where streets were rumored to be made of gold, didn't come as easily as Vijay had imagined, he clung to rules. Rules made him feel safe in the face of our poverty, multiplying like mold on a shower curtain with every loss we suffered.

I once read that feelings of helplessness in one area of our lives, can lead to micromanaging other areas – sometimes to an extreme. After we were robbed, Vijay saw potential danger everywhere and resorted to rituals to counter it. He had us reciting mantras to invoke auspiciousness upon rising, before eating, before exiting the house, before traveling, and before sleeping. At first, Viyay's rituals felt like soft, warm blankets lovingly wrapped around us. Later, they morphed into tight, prickly straight-jackets I struggled to pull off.

Vijay burst into anger or disappointment if I wore my hair down after sunset, looked at him out of one eye, left the curtains open after dusk, or exited our home with my left foot instead of my right. My steps could not sound heavy, my weight could not increase, my hair had to be parted precisely in the middle. Vijay insisted my head not rest on my hand, that I toss out all food prepared before an eclipse, shoo cawing crows off our roof, and under no circumstances was I ever to whistle. There were rules about not falling asleep with our feet touching or staying up later than ten. Rules about not leaving dishes in the sink overnight. Rules about not reading novels. Right before our marriage imploded, Vijay began reprimanding me for attending yoga classes at a school that was not philosophically aligned with his own yoga lineage.

Beyond superstitions and cultural conditioning, I sensed that Vijay's rules were driven by trauma. But how does one expunge fear from an unattended inner child?

Especially one locked inside of a man who is too busy making demands of others to look within? "Therapy is for the weak-minded," he said. Chanting mantras was his solution to everything. In the end, Vijay found it easier to run back to his monastic hermitage in India. So, thirteen years into our marriage, a thriving business, a mortgage, and two kids, Vijay returned to the quiet shores of the sacred River Ganges. From a pink temple on the edge of a green rice patty field, my husband called me full of lamentations that he was a married man. Again!

As I ran out the door to pick our children up from school, Vijay unpacked stories of warm reunions with his ashrama friends, how he felt at home among them, how he wished he could stay there forever. But, what about us? You have a family here! We love you! We just bought a new home! On that day, I don't think anything I could have offered my husband would have compared to the freedom of being a monk. I parked on the side of a corn field, down a sunny, country road and cried my eyes out until a police officer pulled over to check on me. In the back of our blue minivan he spotted soccer balls and kites, in the driver's seat, a disheveled young mother; her heart, nothing but pink pulp chum for piranhas.

When Vijay returned from India his own heart was in full monk-mode. This world, and everything in it, myself included, only worthy of renunciation. As conflicted as ever, Vijay feared the bad karma of divorce. In fact, he had many fears. I watched fear surface in him as fast as flood waters rise during the monsoon season. Vijay feared ghosts. He feared snakes. He feared curses and thieves. Vijay feared reincarnation and what might happen if I didn't chase the crows off our roof. Most of all, Vijay feared love: the love of a woman, the love of family. Things that his monastic training told him were obstacles on the way to transcending this world. You see, I didn't lose my husband to another woman. I lost him to a quest for enlightenment. At least that's what I imagine he felt like on the outside and on the inside, a scared child of war longing for safety, desperate for a world free of anxiety.

Our separation was a disentangling ball of yarn that kept knotting up whichever way you pulled it. The logistics were mind-boggling, the lawyers dizzying. Plus, Vijay and I were the first to divorce in either of our families. His family shunned me, mine reeled with disappointment. Neither were supportive. Inevitably, the road Vijay and I took from "married" to "divorced" was not straight. Instead, it curved up peaks, plunged into dark valleys and had us making sharp U-turns over and over again for a period of years. While I juggled everything to make the transition smooth for the children, Vijay was back to knocking on bamboo poles, listening for safety. Sadly, all he heard was a deep hollow. Even our marriage sounded hollow to him. In the end, all that Vijay and I shared was grief.

Heartbreak can be like a chameleon; taking on different colors every time it's revisited. When I rewind my marriage with Vijay back to the first year, I see two youth in love, happily settled into a rented, cockroach-infested, studio apartment that flooded every time it rained. We held hands as we lay next to each other on a futon we'd rolled out on the linoleum floor. We took turns telling stories from India and Mexico, making each other laugh until the early morning hours when drunks loitered outside our bedroom window. We were newlyweds then, consumed by a naïve certainty that only death could pull us apart. I never imagined that our story would end with Vijay and I both miserable, in a two-story mortgaged home on 20 acres of paradisal pastures and woodlands, sharing a king-sized canopy bed under cathedral ceilings, but not speaking to each other. The pillows between us may as well have been whole galaxies. Outside: owls, crickets, frogs, the sound of the universe continuing to exist—amazingly—even after ours had collapsed with a big crunch.

After our marriage broke, so did I. At least, initially. My stomach turned knots, my body forgot how to sleep, my weight dropped so fast clothes flapped on me like flags in the wind. Vijay's loss unspooled grief from my heart that I had been carrying around from previous losses: the death of my childhood friend, Monica, the deaths of my grandparents, the death of our unborn daughter, Kalindi. For a few weeks, friends flowed in and out of my home bringing baked goods and casserole dishes, offering to drive my boys to school, filling my vases with fresh wildflowers. Elder women in the community were brought in for limpias, with their feathers and copal, their herbal brews, hand drums and healing. I found comfort in their maternal voices, sipped ancestral gifts in their teas. There was no wasting this pain, they said. It has come to teach me something. It was, ultimately, my friend. The snakes they kept seeing on my property were good omens telling them I was ripe for change.

They told me that metamorphosis completely breaks down a caterpillar's body until it's nothing but a soupy liquid. After my own breakdown, making art became my magical primordial soup. While in my grief cocoon, I returned to all the precious things that had sustained me in the past – poetry, crafts, painting, dance – and I set out to remake myself. Especially on rainy days when nostalgia tugged at my heart, I'd cover our kitchen table with art supplies and invite my boys to join me. Together, with cheap finger paints, big sheets of paper and music on the stereo, we made new memories. I wanted my boys to watch me join generations of single mothers who not only knew how to endure pain, but how to befriend it. I wanted them to know that even amidst the rubble you can create joy. And I pictured my Abuelita, as a young widow in her late 20's, teaching her songbirds to sing, filling her kitchen with music. There's a song for everything, she would later say. Find the songs for your life and sing them!

During the time of dissolution and remaking, I found my own songs in Mother Nature; and with them, my own forgotten pulse. After their father moved out, my children and I let our little property go wonderfully wild until pastures sprouted woodlands and wore bouncy, pine-needle coats. We stopped mowing so that wildflowers and thickets overtook our green lawn. Soon rabbits burrowed, moles multiplied, and the land became a midwife to many happy fawns. Spring breezes were perfumed with jasmine, magnolias, and gardenias. We played soccer, climbed trees. Summertime saw us languishing in the shade of live oaks popping blackberries into our mouths, licking warm juice off our fingers. Autumn undressed the maples and birch to the bone; tossing off orange and yellow garments with the help of Northern gales. This was a glorious bonfire season, when the kids and I danced around flames taller than we were. No one yelled at us to come in. In the absence of Vijay's noisy gardening equipment and swinging machete, wilderness took over until mating raptors nested in her limbs, arachnid silks decorated her untamed hair, prowling lynx hunted on her soft mounds. This untamed wilderness was the antithesis of controlling rules. It was trusting that life thrives when you stop trying to dominate it. And, so did we.

It's difficult to pin-point the specific moment I felt things shift within me, but something definitely shifted. In the wilderness, I found the secret to shedding my old skin and growing a new one was to live like the wilderness creatures: in the moment. I stopped thinking of Vijay and nurtured the person I was without him: no longer his wife, but an independent woman, a single mother and creative. Just like the land we lived on, little by little, I revived the dormant sides of myself that had slept through our marriage in order for it to work. These sides poured out of me through painting, dancing, gardening, quilting, crocheting, hiking, yoga, journaling, singing, photography, and more. Creative muses woke me in the middle of the night, taking me into my artistic zone, one project after another. My spirit found many outlets and my voice, many ways to express itself. Part grief, part celebration, this creative drive healed and motivated me even on days that tried to swallow me whole. Like thousands of monarch butterflies simultaneously taking flight out of Michoacán's hilltops, I eventually felt my lost selves taking wing again, scaling mountains, crossing borders – compass set to my own true north.

Note: Names in the story have been changed for privacy purposes.

Luz Schweig ran an international women's poetry journal for ten years, through which she edited and produced five anthologies and a posthumous poetry collection. She has worked as an editor and ghostwriter in a variety of literary projects for 20 years, including as the chief editor of the Somos Xicanas anthology and former staff at Somos en escrito Literary Foundation. Her eclectic range of interests includes designing teacher training programs on yoga philosophy, studying the Tonalamatl, observing a decolonial diet and publishing award winning poetry under a pen name. Luz is on the board of Trustees of the Janavi Held Endowed Poetry and Art Grant, a member of the Raza Unida Party and The Order of the Good Death. She grew up in Mexico City, and today lives on the East Coast with her husband, where they enjoy being grandparents together.

Chapter 9
There is Freedom in saying Fuck You Good-bye!

My high school sweetheart and I spent our teens and early twenties in love. We lost sight of our love because we were too young, and our sense of identity had yet to be unearthed. Instead this devotion flourished into mundane domesticity and raising the daughter we had in our teen-age years. To this day I don't think I ever had "the divorce talk" with my eldest daughter. I never sat her down and explained the tragedy knowing that her father and I would eventually separate, AKA divorce. After all she was shy of turning 6 in the months to come, when our relationship finally came to an end. Even if that meant we were not married legally; down here in the south, we have common-law marriage. Was it as serious as it sounded? I was made to believe that it was.

It was Fall of 2016, as I packed up my things, I would come across mementos and snapshots of our nearly eight years together. That feeling of the, 'no longer' ate at my insides, I could feel it to the pit of my stomach. Wishful promises of 'forever' would no longer culminate our 'happily ever after.' And the saddest part was that my eldest had to live with my crappy choices. She saw it herself, the trauma I succumbed to year after year, yet I pulled through for her. It has been almost a decade, and she holds the same animosity towards me that I once maintained for her father. Mainly because of the control he felt entitled to subject me to. During those times, I would hurl myself into a never-ending loop of a guilt trip and non-stop questioning:

You have to stick this out. No matter what you do, no matter how much he breaks you with words or physical threats, you have to stay for Evelyn. What did I do in life to go through this pain? What do I owe to our daughter? Will I ever feel happiness again?

It was the second day. The day after the attempt—his hands around my throat in a desperate effort to end my life. Thankfully, I was able to escape, with no severe physical evidence—just the emotional distress that replays the scene in my mind every now and then. There is power in no longer feeling tethered to a "marriage" that drained me of energy and stifled my true self and aspirations. By the age of twenty-one, I had enrolled in college—a decision he reluctantly allowed because of the potential financial wealth he believed I could bring once I graduated. He never had to worry about sustaining me financially, as that was never part of his plan. It was the same ol' same ol' — I was tired of it all—the secrets, the neglect, and the toxic family dynamics I had been forced to "marry" into simply because I became pregnant at seventeen. After two years of living together, I became well-versed in the art of lying.

My husband's mother—a self-proclaimed class-A gold-digger—had been married to men from all over the world: Nicaragua, El Salvador, and beyond—her reserved way of conning people. In 2012, we moved into a trailer owned by a "friend." To no one's surprise, the trailer actually belonged to my suegra's secondary lover. The twist? The lover was a woman—married herself, with a whole family setup. Talk about entanglements.

A term I would hold near and dear; since my then-husband seemed to acquire the same foolish facets from his mother. Over the years, I discovered my 'husbands' true colors, that he was a gaslighting king, he held many traits of narcissism, and he made sure I understood the message: A life without him was nonexistent—that death would be my only way out of this god forsaken union.

By the age of ten, I learned que el divorcio was against the Catholic religion, it had to be as bad as the other "d" word— death. To be divorced denoted that someone has committed social suicide; that I had to undergo the all-time low blows no matter what. So, for me to leave a domestic violence relationship even with the possibility of my own death was an act of defiance against everything I was taught to believe. I knew that if I stayed, I would risk losing myself completely, a dawdling deterioration of my will. All of the pieces that make me, uniquely me: My Mexican heritage, my inclination towards women, and my curiosity to gather an understanding about the world around me. So I bit my tongue and endured what I could for the approaching eight years jointly.

He made me feel as if I was simply a nobody in life. That I did not deserve an affirming love or a chance to be loved by someone outside of his shackles. Because I had a child with him, he would repeatedly mention that nobody would ever want me, that my body clung in certain areas & that I was not thin enough for anyone to crave me sexually. There is a thing that happens when someone is continuously breaking each ounce of your self-confidence; I climbed down a hole of self-loathing & depression. This hole of desperation became a familiar place, its walls lined with the echoes of his criticism, and my inner voice soundless & mute. Most days I would stare back at the reflection in the mirror, unbeknownst to me, I no longer recognized the person I had become.

Moving on, I set my sights on the woman I always dreamed of becoming, and slowly but surely I reclaimed pieces of myself that were lost on the way. It was a faint realization to uncover the depths of who I was and an acknowledgment that I no longer had to stay buried forever. With every step forward, I look back and air hug that lost woman, that dreams are not meant to be compromised to fit someone else's mold.

Contrary to how it might seem, post-divorce/post-separation was a journey I owed to myself. Leaving was not just an escape— it was a declaration of my right to exist beyond the confines of what was expected of me. This was when I first discovered the beauty behind self-love. It was a consummation of desire, to be able to live freely without the constraints of someone holding me back.

Crystal Reyes is a Latinx essayist & poet native to Houston and works as an educator. She is a graduate candidate at Bay Path University, working on her MFA in Creative Nonfiction. Her debut poetry collection, Wildflower Blooming was released last Spring. Her essays & other works have been featured in Hip Latina, Entre Magazine, Autostraddle, Text Power Telling & other literary magazines and anthologies. She has received support from the following literary organizations: The Kenyon Review and The Writer's Center. You can follow her work at @Crisreyeswrites

Chapter 10
Unapologetic Survival

When people ask me if physical abuse is worse than mental and emotional abuse I cannot answer them. All abuse is damaging. The day my counselor told me that I have "severe and deep seated PTSD" is the day that I knew healing would be a lifelong task.

I was lucky, my parents and sisters physically stood by me the day I decided I was not going to allow any more abuse. The day my husband, of ten years, dragged me across the living room, into the bedroom, threw me across the bed and threw a dresser drawer at me was the final straw. That drawer missed me and barely missed my five year old son. The same son who was pushed down a week after he learned to walk because "he has to learn what falling down feels like." The same son who was dropped from the arms of his six foot tall father to the floor, to punish me, because I needed "to learn." The same son who, at age five, was on the roof because my husband didn't "want him underfoot while he mowed the lawn."

I did not know a man could be cruel before I was married, at age twenty. Unbeknownst to me I had married a man who married me because he, at age twenty-seven, was "a menace to society" according to our church. The first day I walked into church after our wedding, my husband was walking half a hallway ahead of me. When I asked him to wait he turned, glared in my face, and said "All I ever wanted the first Sunday after being married was to walk into church with a tall beautiful brunette, not you!"
Emotional and mental abuse are difficult to remedy. Nearly impossible in the moment. They eat away at the spirit and mind. Degrade a person's ability to think rationally about self. About love.

I did not leave the day I came home, after a full day of classes and work, and asked my husband if he was okay and his response was "No! I flunked all of my classes and it is your fault because all I can think of every minute of every day is how fat you are!" I did not leave when he told me "You have hippo hips and elephant heels," "You are childish," "You are frigid." Instead, I internalized my shortcomings. Placed less value on my wellbeing. I began to see myself as less than, not good enough, fat, incapable, stupid, ugly, and unworthy of happiness.

I was lucky, he never actually hit me. He always had a job. He attended church. He was a handsome man.

I was lucky, but not aware enough of the signs of love bombing (my first husband was not a love bomber) to avoid a second marriage of violence that lasted less than a third as long as the first and packed a mightier punch.

I was lucky, the police officer who interviewed me, my five children, and my father who had driven us to Alternatives to Violence (ATV), was a father of seven. He and his partner stood up for us. Those officers held my second husband at bay for hours and checked in with the judge every thirty minutes throughout the day so that they could make sure that I got a hearing that day.

The moment they spoke with the judge I was driven to the courthouse by two ATV volunteers and I sat next to the judge in the witness stand for nearly three hours. The judge asked me question after question and those two women, earth angels, held strength in their eyes so that every single time I looked up they were there.

Those two police officers did not have to take a personal interest in our plight, but they did. My parents did not have to put themselves at risk to protect us, but they did. Friends did not have to come to the house at the drop of a hat and pick up the family pets, but they did. It took a lot of strength to leave and I did not do it alone. It was a terrifying, exhausting, heartbreaking day. It was my thirty-sixth birthday and I spent it with my children, in a safe house.

The safe house had food, and beds, enough for all six of us to sleep in the same room, a necessity. The safe house had a backyard with a fence high enough to hide my children as they played. When my children came inside, they felt safe, they told me about abuse that had been hidden from me. It was classic. My second husband had told the children that I knew he was beating them. He was smart. He knew not to place any marks that would show. Hidden bruises under pants and sleeves. My thirty-sixth birthday is the day that broke me.

It didn't break me the day the cops called to say they had arrested him with two handguns and three shopping bags full of ammunition. It didn't break me the day he hit me hard enough to knock all of the teeth on the right side of my face loose. I lost part of my hearing that day. Part of my eyesight. It didn't break me the day he tried to kill me as I prayed for it to be quick.

My six year old son saved my life when he, terrified and courageous, snuck upstairs from his hiding space in a downstairs bedroom, and faced the man who was killing his mother. Seeing my son's face flipped a switch in my husband. He stopped. Crumpled into a heap. Cried. The day I found out that my second husband had beaten my son broke me. The day I found out he had thrown my other son into a wall broke me. And years later, when yet another one of my sons thanked me for marrying his dad, saving him from being the target of his father's abuse which he had suffered for nearly six years, including being stabbed in the bicep with a steak knife at age four, broke me.

The divorce was nineteen years ago and my heart races as I write these words but I am not shaking, I am not crying, and I am not being abused and neither are my children.

Being hit, or degraded, or manipulated, or neglected, or pushed over, or being a pawn in a dangerous game of cat and mouse is not okay. Sometimes there are solutions that can and do make continuing in a marriage worthwhile.

Couples counseling worked for awhile in my first marriage and then one day it didn't.

It was three weeks to the day after the second counselor we saw asked me "Do you know how to call 911?" "Do your kids know how to call 911?" that my first husband became physically abusive with me. This was after years of emotional abuse. The real kicker is that his boss is the one who told him he needed to hit me in order to "take control." Fortunately my first husband did not hit me. I believe it could have been the next step in an established pattern. The end of my first marriage marked the beginning of learning to balance what was best for our children with our own emotional needs. We failed sometimes. However, we built, not without the help of family and friends, a relationship that allowed us to raise all of our children (including those who joined us through subsequent marriages) as siblings. Leaving my second marriage was more difficult in many ways. I felt powerless and blindsided by a relationship that I thought would include love and security. I did find the strength to leave due to my own stubborn desire to protect the children and through help from other people. First, a friend who saw something that I did not shared her own experience about leaving her abusive marriage with me. She emphasized the importance of stashing away money and I started hiding money between the pages of books. My second husband didn't read so I knew it was a safe place for financial freedom to hide.

Another friend, a fellow violist in the symphony, saw something I didn't and told me that the guys in the university marching band were only a phone call away if I wanted to get out. The day I left, my friend called his mother for advice on my behalf. She was a counselor with experience. He drove my family to safety and bought us groceries for dinner. On top of the groceries was a box of herbal tea that my friend had purchased so that I could "find a place of calm" as my children slept. He hid my car to assure our safety that night. I was lucky.

Most importantly, and I recognize that I am fortunate in this aspect of my experience, my family sacrificed a lot. My parents gave us safe spaces, paid legal fees, a lot of them, and loved us. My mother provided home-cooked meals every Sunday, even after working a full week herself and raising her own children, she provided us nourishment and home. Safe, loving, comfortable, nourishing, home. I was lucky. I owe so much to others. When my second husband was arrested with guns and ammunition, an officer, my sister's neighbor, called her and said "Go get your sister NOW." He did this knowing that I had to be the person to remove the guns from the truck so they would not be returned to my husband.

Two separate Bishops in the church we attended provided food, financial assistance, and support. I suspect that at least one of these men used his own resources to assist us.

My university professor who, when I had a complete mental breakdown in her office, called the counseling services and kindly, wisely, forced me to speak to someone with the credentials to help me find the road to mental and physical wellness and safety.

The police department and local judge were our protectors without question. I was told by one of our local police officers that he and his colleagues had never seen "such a comprehensive protective order issued by a judge" In fact, they asked if they could borrow one of the copies that my children and I carried everywhere with us. The officer wanted to show the order to other police officers in the stadium where I worked. They all wanted to see this unicorn of a protective order "with their own eyes."

The men and women in law enforcement watched over my children and over me with eagle eyes as I worked.

They surrounded my house, a circle of protection, when my husband showed up at the door despite the order of protection. They cleared my house after my husband broke in, put dog poop on my son's bed, dumped out dresser drawers, left a vile letter on my pillow next to his mutilated wedding band, and stole my jewelry.

I was surrounded by people who helped me. My attorneys were not only my legal counsel, they gifted my children and me with a river rafting trip so that we could have a place to go where we didn't have to look over our shoulders. A respite, an adventure, a moment of peace. They cared about us and did so not without toll. In fact, my divorce was the last divorce case they ever took on.

It took a community but most importantly, it took me having the courage to ask for help.
If you are in a dangerous situation you are not without help.

You can ask for help. Please ask for help. There are resources available. Alternatives to Violence. Churches. Neighbors. Strangers in the right place at the right time. Please know that you deserve a life free from abuse. You deserve a chance to live in peace.

When we are little we learn pattern recognition. Apple, circle, snail, apple circle, snail, apple, circle…what comes next? Snail!" "Yay!" "You got it!" When we are living in an abusive relationship the pattern is there but it hides in innuendo, gaslighting, love bombing, and so much more. In fact, even though I had learned some of the patterns in the midst of my marriages, I did not see the bigger picture until later. I have written poems about my experience.

Was the process of writing the poems healing? Maybe. A step on the road to feeling whole? Certainly. When these poems took their places on the pages of my book, Gamut Eclectic & Mundane: Life Perspectives, truth emerged.

I was concerned about having several poems in the book about the same place, situation, and moment, but the poems showed the harrowing truth of abuse from several angles and I saw patterns that I had missed when in the midst of the trauma.

There is still a hole in the back of my bedroom door from my husband's head. It is no longer my room. But the hole lives there. For now. A reminder:

another time

the night you put your head
through the bedroom
door

is marked with a hole
the size of your forehead

wide and jagged

a calendar
a journal entry
a timeline hash

it is still there

a gaping mouth
with nothing left to say

I remember that night with a surreal clarity. It used to make me shake inside. Internal vibrato. Hard to breathe. I held back tears. I felt that if tears began they would never end. One time I fell asleep crying and woke up in the morning with tears still streaming down my face. Heartache.

Heartbreak. Trauma. Healing tears rolling down my cheeks to a wet pillow. I survived. You can survive. It does get better.

There have been days when I can't stop thinking about the abuse. There are days now when I don't think of the abuse at all. The space between these days is wider than it used to be.

raw

the day he put his head through the door
was not the same day
he tried to put his head
through the mirror

it was not the day he screamed in my face
until I passed out

it was not the day he gave me roses

it was not the day
he brought me a new puppy

it feels like the same day
it feels like yesterday
& a century ago

my cheek still aches
where his hand met my face

my eyes do not focus anymore

the one I loved most hit me the hardest
reached into my chest
grabbed my heart
& ripped it

from between
my ribs

blood
drips
from his
chin

& the bite he took
was big enough
to gag us
both

Patterns become apparent. Abuse. Gift. Abuse. Love bombing. Abuse. Attention. Abuse. Living creatures who depend
on me. Abuse…

battleskars

i cannot —

rub away
print of hand
on this cheek

mend
hamburger skin
in this mouth

replicate
sturdiness
of this jaw

&
the
door
asks
through
splintered
mahogany

why did he hit you—

put his fist
where it did not
belong?

i answer—

love
inquires
of the devil

a cheater
& a liar

as though he
has the answers

    Do you see the patterns? Do you know the patterns?
Yelled in my face until I passed out. Flowers. Bold chested
me into a wall until I couldn't breathe. A puppy. Broke the
kitchen chair in one hard slam because he didn't like something I said. Sapphire bracelet. Abuse. Dinner out. Abuse.
A new outfit . Abuse. A night of attention with me at the
center.
    Interestingly, as long as the abuse involved me it

was solved by these patterns. I did not value myself enough to leave. I did not think that I could function on my own. Slowly, I began to see the patterns more clearly and I gathered the money hiding in books, packed up my children, and left.

As in every story of abuse, these words on this paper are only part of the story, the tip of the iceberg, the corner edge. You may be thinking to yourself "What was the straw that broke the camel's back?" The answer is my children. He laid his hands on my children. He put my six-year-old son in a position no child should ever be in. That of a protector and savior. He beat and bruised my son. He hit my daughter and son with a belt so hard that they have scars nineteen years later that still mark their skin. He threw my son into a wall.

I left on November 5, 2005. Filed for divorce on November,7, 2005. I was legally divorced on December 19, 2005. For me, in my situation, divorce was the answer. The next step was surviving after divorce. But how?
I learned quickly that the moment I got dressed in the morning I had to put on my shoes and tie the laces tight. I did not un-tie those shoes until I had accomplished everything I had to do each day. I slept with all of my children in one room because they were too scared to sleep alone. A bunk bed, a trundle bed, a mattress on the floor, a locked door, and a six year old who built a booby trap behind that door every single night, for months.
Fear was the fabric of the coats we wore. The children received stuffed animals and cell phones from ATV. Both were important, one was lifesaving. Both of the schools that my children attended were in soft lock down for several days due to my husband attempting to enter the schools to collect the children and "take them somewhere you (I) will never see them again."

To this day if I hear a particular cordless landline phone ring on a movie or TV show I can't breathe. If I hear a truck that sounds like his, see a purple Toyota, hear a gunshot, my mind retreats to its ancient brain and the perceived "Danger!" is met by trauma response.

It is better than it used to be. It is not all better. I will continue to work toward wellness, wholeness, self-discovery and balance for the remainder of my life. The good news is that it does get better. I can look in the mirror with compassion for me. Love for me. Acceptance of me.

Where I used to see an ugly, stupid, incapable, fat, worthless, broken woman, I now see a capable, beautiful, fluffy, loving human being. There are still days when my mind returns to a place of pain and darkness but I don't linger there. I am learning to see from a new perspective. It has taken a lot of work.

I started the process of healing many years ago by reciting mantras in my head while swimming laps. "I am beautiful," "I am strong," "I am capable," for an hour every day, five days a week. I forced myself to find one thing I liked about myself each day and recite it to myself in the mirror and eventually I worked up to three good things. Every single day.

It took a long time but one day being kind to myself was no longer forced. I stopped hating myself, blaming myself, punishing myself. I began to know my value. My worth. I am here to remind you that you are valuable. You are worthwhile, beautiful, wanted, needed, and loved.

love in a mirror

I wake up
every
single
morning

(on nights I actually sleep)

drag myself to the bathroom
& drop my clothes

on
         the
    floor

look in the mirror
& lean in–

run my fingers over a scar
on my cheek

chant "I am beautiful"
"I am smart"
"I am capable"
"I am deserving
of
my
love"

   Life moves on with or without us. It is okay to
mourn. It is okay to feel betrayed, angry, furious. It is okay
to feel weary, exhausted, worn down. It is also okay to laugh.
To smile. To find joy. My father gave me a blessing in the
midst of the trauma. I consider it a gift. He said; "Someday

you will find more joy in life than you ever thought possible."

That night, as I put my head on my pillow, tears streamed down my face as they did nearly every night and a single ladybug crawled up my wall until it was directly across from me. That ladybug rested awhile and tears of sorrow were mixed with tears of love and joy. My parents called me "ladybug" as a small child. That little red and black insect represented undying, unconditional love in the midst of harrowing pain and anguish.

I now look for joy and I find it. Regularly. It is in the clouds, my grandchildren's eyes, a white feather in my path, a perfect flower, a towering and majestic old tree. I can find joy almost everywhere now. It is abundant. I wear clothes that make me feel happy. Colorful.

I unapologetically seek out people, places, experiences, and things that I enjoy. and I am here, Alive.
When people ask me if physical abuse is worse than mental and emotional abuse I cannot answer them. All abuse is damaging. The day my counselor told me that I have "severe and deep seated PTSD" is the day I knew that healing would be a lifelong task. It is possible to survive and find joy again.

End note: Both of the men I divorced have worked to become better men today than they were when I was married to them. They have become more positive figures in the lives of their children. They are grandparents who love their grandchildren. They are spouses who treat their wives differently than they treated me. People can change. People do change. It is still okay that I chose to preserve my life and the lives of my children years ago through divorce.

Cherice Cameron is a multifaceted artist and writer whose poetry delves into the complexities of human experience. Her published collection, Gamut Eclectic & Mundane: Life Perspectives, showcases her keen observation and lyrical voice. Beyond the written word, Cherice expresses her creativity as an editor, orchestra director, and musician, as well as through her visual art. As a devoted mother and grandmother, she understands the intricacies of family and relationships. Cherice finds inspiration in the natural world, the thrill of travel, and the joy of constant discovery. Her contributions to When Divorce is the Right Answer reflect her compassionate understanding of life's challenging transitions and the courage required to forge a new path.

Final Note

We hope you found some courage and strength through this anthology. The best thing we can say to you is that you are the most important person in your life, so please take care of yourself. Get the help you need to be free of the past. You deserve happiness, joy, but most importantly you deserve peace of mind. You are not alone. Find strength in friends, community, and loved ones. Take this opportunity to discover the beauty you carry inside you. You matter and you can have an incredible beautiful life, if you would just let go and discover your true self. Sending you so much love and hope.

Publisher's Note

Daxson publishing was created to help marginalized artists and their allies publish their work, so the world can hear their voice. The vision for this publishing house is to help people get their work out there, and not have them struggle finding their way through the publishing process. Everyone's voice deserves to be heard, and we are here to help. If you are interested in submitting a manuscript, email daxsonpublishing@gmail.com.

Support our cause! Buy our books at daxsonpublishing.com.

www.ingramcontent.com/pod-product-compliance
Lightning Source LLC
Chambersburg PA
CBHW061737120626
46550CB00005B/1816